Ellis Nelson has thought longer and better about Christian education than anyone else on the planet. After a lifetime as a distinguished church educator, this book offers what I take to be his "final answer" to the crisis of church education in a secular culture. Nelson thinks in large terms of a new cultural context wherein the infrastructure of church nurture has largely disintegrated. Nelson urges that in the twenty-first century fresh ways of nurture, socialization, and incorporation must be undertaken with careful intentionality. He focuses on the informal influences of home, family, and church community and on the formal influences of educational and liturgic enterprises. Nelson knows how "up hill" such a venture now is; but he also knows, full well, that Christian nurture matches profound human hungers, and so we do not lose heart. Nelson as a practical theologian thinks practically in a way that will support and summon other educational practitioners. His "final word" is a splendid, powerful, grace-filled word.

—**Walter Brueggemann**
Columbia Theological Seminary

Ellis Nelson has spent a lifetime thinking deeply about how children, youth, and adults are nurtured in Christian faith and its way of life. This new book is full of wisdom concerning this crucial question. The congregation as a whole is the key. Parents, pastors, and teachers all have crucial roles to play. Nelson shows how we can all work together to nurture Christian disciples in the twenty-first century.

—**Craig Dykstra**
Senior Vice President, Religion Division
Lilly Endowment, Inc.

Growing Up Christian is a wise, practical, and highly readable book. Ellis Nelson explains with remarkable clarity why current strategies for nurturing disciples are inadequate and examines with keen insight the influence of parents and congregations in the development of the idea of God among children and youth and their roles in nurturing young people as disciples of Jesus Christ. This is an important book for pastors, Christian educators, parents, and congregational leaders concerned about the future of the faith of our children and the vitality of the faith of our congregations. I especially recommend they read it together.

—**Charles R. Foster**
Professor of Religion and Education emeritus
Candler School of Theology
Emory University

GROWING UP CHRISTIAN

Smyth & Helwys Publishing, Inc.
6316 Peake Road
Macon, Georgia 31210-3960
1-800-747-3016
©2008 by Smyth & Helwys Publishing
All rights reserved.
Printed in the United States of America.

Images (pages 59-60) from *Acquiring Our Image of God*, by Martin A. Lang, Ph.D.
Copyright © 1983 by Martin A. Lang. Paulist Press, Inc., New York/Mahwah, NJ.
Reprinted by permission of Paulist Press, Inc. www.paulistpress.com

The paper used in this publication meets the minimum requirements of
American National Standard for Information Sciences—
Permanence of Paper for Printed Library Materials.
ANSI Z39.48–1984. (alk. paper)

Library of Congress Cataloging-in-Publication Data

Nelson, Carl Ellis, 1916-
Growing up Christian:
A congregational strategy for nurturing disciples
by C. Ellis Nelson.
p. cm.
ISBN 978-1-57312-523-9 (pbk. : alk. paper)
1. Church work with children.
2. Children—Religious life.
3. Christian education of children.
4. Church work with teenagers.
5. Teenagers—Religious life.
6. Christian education of teenagers.
I. Title.
BV639.C4N45 2008
253—dc22

2008024266

Growing Up
CHRISTIAN

A Congregational Strategy for Nurturing Disciples

C. Ellis Nelson

Also by C. Ellis Nelson

Growth in Grace and Knowledge

Helping Teenagers Grow Morally: A Guide for Adults

Christian Education: Responsibility for Moral Decision Making

How Faith Matures

Congregations: Their Power to Form and Transform (editor)

Don't Let Your Conscience Be Your Guide

Using Evaluation in Theological Education

Conscience: Theological and Psychological Perspectives (editor)

Issues Facing Christian Educators

Where Faith Begins

What's Right

Love and the Law

To Lewis Joseph Sherrill
Christian educator par excellence
who embodied Christian beliefs and lifestyle

ACKNOWLEDGMENTS

Chapters 2 and 3 of this book in their original form were given as the Robert F. Jones lectures in Christian education at Austin Presbyterian Theological Seminary. I appreciate the invitation from President Robert M. Shelton, the faculty, and the Board of Trustees to give these lectures and for the many privileges they have afforded me as a research professor. My wife, Nancy, used her knowledge of Protestant churches as well as her editing skills to clarify the purposes of those lectures.

Prescott H. Williams, Jr., Professor Emeritus of Old Testament Languages and Archaeology at Austin Presbyterian Theological Seminary, in addition to conversing with me about the purpose of this book, made helpful suggestions about the text. Alison Riemersma corrected the manuscript while she typed it several times. Sandra Seamans carefully checked the biblical references and the quotations used to support the ideas being discussed. Maria Collins and Emily Summerfield reviewed the text as they inserted changes in the final version of the book. My dependence on these people for their help in preparing this book for publication is gratefully acknowledged.

—C. Ellis Nelson

TABLE OF CONTENTS

INTRODUCTION

The strategy most congregations use to encourage children and teenagers to become disciples of Jesus Christ is inadequate. This is so because this strategy was formed in the 1800s in response to an American culture that no longer exists. In the 1800s Christianity in various forms was communicated to the rising generation through the *McGuffey Readers* used in the public schools; through church congregations, which were the major community institutions; and through parents who took responsibility for family prayers and conversations about how to live as a Christian. Sunday school was developed as a way to support what the public schools and families were doing and to teach the special theological beliefs of the congregation about such matters as the proper form of baptism.

Our culture is more secular, individualistic, commercial, competitive, and more oriented to the power of science to make life interesting and enjoyable. These cultural values influence our children through television, computers, cell phones, public schools, athletic events, magazines, radio, and newspapers. This general description of our cultural situation is assumed throughout the book. At the end of chapter 1, I cite recent studies to show how some of these cultural values have influenced the religious beliefs of teenagers.

Given the cultural values of the twenty-first century, how can congregations more effectively nurture disciples of Jesus Christ? The answer to this question is *not* to propose a new theory of Christian education, to criticize the Sunday school or other church-sponsored educational programs, to offer a new curriculum, or to promote a different method of classroom teaching. These elements of Christian education are important and necessary but are not sufficient for our cultural environment.

A clue to what is sufficient comes from the Bible; almost all of the biblical accounts of people who believed in God lived in a society that did not support such a belief. This clue is recorded in the Shema, which Hebrews were to repeat when they got up in the morning and when they went to bed at night (Deut 6:4-9). The first priority is that members of the community (Israel) are to "love the Lord your God with all your heart, and with all your soul [self], and with all your might." The second priority is for parents to nurture their children in the home by reciting the beliefs of Israel and by applying them to events that happen during the day.

The Apostle Paul used the same strategy. When Paul shared the gospel with adults, he baptized the entire family and brought them into a congregation. Paul expected the congregation to nurture the adults, as all his letters to congregations include Christian beliefs and the style of life expected of believers. Parents were responsible for the Christian nurture of their baptized children (Acts 16:25-35).

The biblical clue about nurturing disciples is more than a strategy. The Shema required that followers love God with their whole being. When Jesus was asked to give the greatest commandment, he quoted the Shema and then added, "you should love your neighbor as yourself" (Mark 12:29-31). The word "love," used for our relation to God and neighbor, describes a relationship and therefore involves our emotions, attitudes, desires, and affections. These aspects of our selves are formed out of relationships with other people and our mental images of God. Thus, the word "nurture" seems to be a better word for our efforts to relate children and teenagers to God than the word "educate," which often is connected to knowledge about God. Knowledge about God is important but must not be substituted for a concern to do God's will. At the end of chapter 3, I record the story of nationally known men who, although active church members, were mature adults before they learned about the will of God.

The question, "What can a congregation do to make its efforts to nurture disciples more effective?" is answered in two parts. Part 1 describes the pattern of influences that form our images of God. Chapter 1 explains why the strategy of the 1800s was so successful and why it is not sufficient for the 2000s. Until this history is understood, congregations will not be interested in changing their nurturing strategy.

Chapter 2 describes the critical importance of parents in forming their children's images of God. This information is significant in that the researchers do not attempt to prove anything about God: they simply show how parents' interaction with their children causes children to form ideas of what God is like.

Chapter 3 illustrates how older children begin to think about the ideas of God they received from their parents and other sources of influence such as Sunday school. This chapter ends with examples of how some people move into adulthood with knowledge of God and enrollment in a congregation but have little understanding about how the love of God relates to their vocation.

Given the way culture and family influence the rising generation, Part 2 outlines a strategy for nurturing disciples that utilizes a pattern of influence in harmony with Christian faith. Chapter 4 provides examples of how a congregation can be a powerful subculture that defines and supports a Christian way of life. The parts of Sunday worship service—hymns, Scripture, prayers, and sermons— are distinctly different from the values of our secular society. The issue, therefore, is for congregations to accentuate and celebrate the beliefs that make them a unique community.

Chapter 5 continues this line of analysis by noting how congregations have an ethos or characteristics that both define and support the meaning of Christianity for adults. This ethos is formed and communicated by the interaction of adults as they talk and work together in the life and work of the congregation. Such interaction is a dynamic form of interpreting Christianity between adults and from parents to their children. This natural ongoing process produces this question: "Are adults involved in a systematic study of the Bible and theology so their interaction will help them 'grow in grace and knowledge of our Lord and Savior Jesus Christ' (2 Pet 3-18)?"

Chapter 6 turns attention to how the worship and sermon influence the lives of all who attend. Hymns, prayers, and announcements all have a positive effect, but the sermon is the most direct effort to nurture disciples. Some of the value of the sermon slips away because there is seldom any way for adults to process the meaning of the sermon with other adults. There are some ways,

however, that a pastor can bridge the gap between what is proclaimed and the life situation of church members.

Chapter 7 is devoted to the critical importance of instruction for
all age groups in the traditional Sunday school or in any other
church-sponsored agency of instruction. This strategy of nurture puts
highest priority on adult instruction. Why? Because adults are the
officers of the congregation who help set its mission; adults are the
Sunday school teachers and youth group leaders; and parents are the
teachers and models of Christianity in the family.

At the end of this book is a discussion guide. It is my hope that
officers and other congregational leaders will form a group to spend
eight weeks studying this book in order to assay the strategy they are
using to nurture disciples and to decide ways they can make their
nurturing process more effective.

[Part One]

PATTERNS OF INFLUENCE

Chapter 1

WHY THE STRATEGY OF THE 1800S IS INADEQUATE FOR THE 2000S

"PATTERNS OF INFLUENCE"[1]

The culture of a people includes everything considered important for their well-being, such as ideas, rules, laws, customs, religion, and family traditions. Culture influences our beliefs and habits because it becomes a part of our life the day we are born.[2] Unless our cultural values are challenged by an alternative way to live, they will influence what we think and do throughout our lives. Because culture is so deep within us, it is difficult to understand its source and power.

The easiest way to realize how culture has shaped our lives is to visit or live in a culture different from the one in which we were raised. Another way to grasp the influence of culture is to study the historical account of how people lived in a certain time and place. I have used this historical method in the following story of what life was like in America during the 1800s. As the story unfolds, note the "patterns of influence" that shaped the mentality of most of the population. Also note the educational strategy developed by congregations during that century.

The second section of this chapter takes each of the major agencies that shaped the lives of people in the 1800s and first part of the 1900s and identifies how those sources of influence have changed.

The 1800s: A Formative Era

At the beginning of the 1800s, the United States was a small rural nation with a population of about 5.3 million in an area of about 864,746 square miles. Only six cities had a population of 8,000 people.[3] After the Civil War, America became more urban, more industrialized, and by 1900 grew to a population of 76 million occupying 3 million square miles of land. Almost one-third of this population were immigrants or children of foreign-born parents.[4] The expansion of territory, increase in population, and development of both rural and urban lifestyles make for a complex 100-year history. In our focus on the development of a Protestant educational strategy during these years, we can identify the major causative factors shaping a strategy that began in the 1800s and continued into the early 1900s. The factors considered here include ethos, cultural values, public schools and religion, mass media, congregations, families, Sunday schools, and higher education.

Ethos

A historian said that to understand a historical era one must identify the "spell" under which the people lived. A "spell" means the spirit of the age or something like "unargued assumptions" about life that describe the deep-seated mentality children absorb from their culture.

The "spell" or ethos of the 1800s was an evangelical Protestantism known as the Second Great Awakening. It started in the early 1800s in Kentucky and Tennessee as well as at Yale University in the form of revivals. It caused masses of people to confess faith in Jesus Christ as their Lord and Savior; it created new denominations; it enlivened older churches; and it permeated almost every aspect of society. The term "evangelical" labels a form of Protestantism that stresses a personal experience with Jesus Christ as Lord and Savior.[5]

Revivals and their effects on people, churches, and society continued throughout the 1800s. They occurred under a tent to attract people who had no religion, and they were often scheduled in churches to re-evangelize the faith of members. Revivalists such as Charles Finney (1792–1875) attracted large crowds in the mid-1800s, and also trained people to preach and conduct revivals.[6]

After the Civil War the nation became more industrialized. Evangelical church leaders saw young men coming to urban areas to engage in work different from that on the farm and to embark on a lifestyle to which they were not accustomed. The Young Men's Christian Association (YMCA), which started in England in response to industrialization, came to America and quickly became an agency for evangelizing young men. Dwight L. Moody (1837–1899), having moved to Chicago in order to make more money selling shoes, became actively engaged in the YMCA. In 1861 he gave up his business to devote himself full time to the YMCA. By 1875 he was an experienced evangelist, having conducted revivals in England attended by more than 2.5 million people. Moody made revivals a huge public event, involving careful advance planning, adequate funding, publicity, use of celebrities on the platform, and massed choirs under the direction of Ira D. Sankey. In 1886, at a conference at Northfield, Massachusetts, Moody's center for college students, more than a hundred students volunteered to become foreign missionaries. This event was the beginning of the Student Volunteer Movement that, prior to WWII, enlisted thousands of college students for evangelistic work around the world.[7]

Church historians use different terms to describe the "spell" that characterized America in the 1800s, but they agree that evangelical Protestantism defined the religious outlook of that century. Robert T. Handy's history is of special significance. Handy writes that evangelicals made up the "dominant religious subculture of nineteenth-century America. Moreover, Protestants had a view of what the American culture should be, which they included in their interpretation of religion."[8] Handy illustrated this combination of religion and culture with this quotation from Horace Bushnell's "Barbarism, the First Danger."[9]

> The wilderness shall bud and blossom as the rose before us; and we will not cease, till a christian nation throws up its temples of worship on every hill and plain; till knowledge, virtue and religion, blending their dignity and their healthful power, have filled our great country with a manly and happy race of people, and the bands of a complete christian commonwealth are seen to span the continent.

Winthrop S. Hudson summarizes the history of America during the 1800s in the following paragraph:

> Protestantism had been the dominant religious and cultural force in the United States from the beginning, but by the middle of the nineteenth century it had established undisputed sway over almost all aspects of the national life. It was a Protestant America that had been fashioned by the churches; and the influence of the churches, as has been suggested in an earlier chapter, extended far beyond their somewhat narrowly defined membership. The vast majority of Americans, even when not actual communicants, regarded themselves as "adherents" of one church or another; and among the populace at large the patterns of belief and conduct—both private and public, individual and corporate—were set by the churches.

Although Hudson believed that the above assessment could be documented in many ways, he selected four major matters for consideration. First, during the mid-1800s the religious press grew more rapidly than the secular press. Second, the public's response to revivals was positive and revivals were well attended. Third, the transition from private or church schools to tax-supported public schools took place rather smoothly because Protestant religion was being taught in the public schools. Fourth, almost all colleges founded prior to the Civil War were established by churches, thus providing a religiously educated leadership for society.[10]

Martin E. Marty's *Protestants in the United States* is significant because he wrote as a social historian, giving special attention to the way various groups of people lived in relation to their social/political situation. From that perspective, Marty's way of expressing the "spell" that captured the mind of Protestants was to write that they were determined to form a "Righteous Empire."[11]

Harriet Martineau, an Englishwoman who was a sociologist, a feminist, a political liberal, and a Unitarian, visited the United States from 1834 to 1836. She was critical of the churches, for she found few ministers who understood what she thought were the moral implications of Christianity, and she considered popular Protestantism "superstition." She was astonished that in a nation where religion was optional, almost no one rejected it![12]

Cultural Values

Ethos, as the "spell" of an era, does not mean that everyone agrees with it but that everyone is aware of the way it becomes expressed in cultural values. When cultural values become hardened into customs and laws, they represent what most people consider to be important for the welfare of society and what they want to pass on to the next generation. This "oughtness" of cultural values is important for the church's nurturing strategy. Protestants in the 1800s, for example, considered Sabbath observance a command from God. This belief became a value resulting in laws regulating business and entertainment activity on Sunday. In other areas such as sexual activity, marriage and divorce, gambling, and use of alcohol, the values held by Protestants also became laws. When the church's values take the form of social customs or laws, society becomes an agency that teaches the church's moral code.

Public Schools and Religion

The first words of the first amendment to the constitution (1791) are, "Congress shall make no laws respecting an establishment of religion, or prohibiting the free exercise thereof." This separation of church and state did not have an immediate effect on general education because tax-supported schools did not become widespread until Horace Mann and others began to promote them. It was not until about 1860 that the principle of universal, compulsory, secular, tax-supported schools was established.[13]

Establishing the principle of secular public schools did not mean that the evangelical Protestant ethos evaporated from the schools. Teachers, who probably were Christian, would display their faith and morals informally throughout the day. Schools were opened with prayer and Bible reading. The primary source of Christian instruction was *McGuffey's Readers*. Written by a Presbyterian minister and first published in 1836, the *Readers* reflected a Calvinist theology in the prayers and included a selection of biblical passages and stories to cultivate the virtues of honesty, obedience, kindness, thrift, industry, patriotism, cleanliness, and curiosity. From 1836 to 1850, seven million copies were sold, and by 1890 the *Readers* were used for teaching reading in thirty-seven states. Four out of every five children who learned to read in public schools from 1836 to the early 1900s did so with *McGuffey's Readers*.[14]

Mark Sullivan summarized his study of textbooks used in the 1800s with this sentence: "As education broadened with the addition . . . of arithmetic, grammar, geography, and history, the religious tradition was carried on in all the textbooks in which it could be included appropriately." Even chemistry, biology, and botany textbooks related the material to the existence or the power and wisdom of God.[15]

Mass Media

Mass media is an important aspect of modern culture because it cannot be easily ignored. It either silently and slowly shapes the mentality of people or it forces people to resist the messages it contains.

The mass media in the 1800s consisted of newspapers, journals, leaflets, and books. Books were expensive and newspapers were available primarily in urban areas. Churches, schools, and colleges were the institutions that informed the public. Mark Sullivan, for example, reports that leading citizens in the early 1900s who had their formative years in the latter part of the 1800s cited *McGuffey's Readers* as having the most influence on their lives. Sullivan judges that probably "nine out of ten average Americans" got the literature they read from what the children brought home from school.[16]

As mentioned earlier, one of Hudson's reasons for judging that Protestants dominated American culture was that during the mid-1800s the religious press grew more rapidly than the secular press, both in the number of periodicals and in circulation. Hudson says Whitney R. Cross, who studied central and western New York, "found it difficult to understand how they [religious journals] could have had such wide appeal." Cross finally decided "laymen read and relished the theological treatises" they contained.[17]

Congregations

The evangelical Protestantism that characterized American culture in the 1800s radiated from established congregations and also formed clusters of congregations that became new denominations. Congregations were not only the centers of religious life, but they also assumed leadership roles in most communities. This was achieved by their size, the education of their ministers, which was on a par with that of lawyers and doctors, and their support of public schools and other civic enterprises for the welfare of the community.

The above paragraph contains a critical element of Protestant strategy often overlooked today—the Christian nurture of adults through active congregational involvement. Participation in congregational life was considered to be the way to form adults' beliefs and lifestyle. Most congregations had strict standards for membership and ways of deciding whether an adult violated those standards. A foreign visitor to Lexington, Kentucky, in 1835 reported churches with 200 to 300 members having Sunday attendance four times their memberships.[18]

The general religious influence of society plus the intense, serious nature of participation in a congregation formed the life of adults. The adults were motivated and competent to explain their faith to their children, to teach in the Sunday school, to serve as officers in the congregation, and to share their faith with other adults in the community.

Families

The church's influence on adults who were parents was a major element in its strategy for Christian nurture. Throughout the 1800s, even toward the close of that century when urban life became more common, the nuclear family continued to be the typical type of family.[19] Statistical data about the family size, income, and other facts are not available prior to 1900. What we have are letters, magazines, laws, church pronouncements, diaries, books on what the family should be like, books of stories to read to children, and reports about family life from visitors to America.[20] We can, however, gain enough from these sources to understand how the home was the place where children of church members first learned about God and what God expected of them.

The best-known visitor to the United States was Alexis de Tocqueville. Writing about his visit in the early 1830s, he noted there were "innumerable multitudes of sects in the United States"; yet "all of the sects . . . belong to the great unity of Christendom, and Christian morality is everywhere the same." He also observed that

Christianity had a great influence on government and on the home as a place where citizens found "order and peace."[21]

The education of girls, according to de Tocqueville, was like that of boys; it took place in an environment of Protestant teaching and under the direct tutelage of their mothers. The home, therefore, was the place where girls learned their role as wives and mothers—about the only roles known to women prior to the Civil War. Boys, like girls, stage by stage acquired the role they were to play under the supervision of their fathers and moved into marriage in their late teen years.[22]

We must not assume that family life in the 1800s, especially prior to the Civil War, was ideal. Arthur Calhoun has provided an abundance of data from various magazines, notes from Europeans who visited America, and letters to indicate that life was hard and that marriage was often a matter of convenience and necessity rather than a loving relationship. But even so, Calhoun records the status of religion in the following sentence: "In 1855 Schaff said that table prayer was almost universal; and daily family worship the rule—at least in religious circles."[23]

It is in "religious circles" that we find the power of family faith and practice being inculcated in children. The best and most enduring explanation of family religion in the 1800s is Horace Bushnell's *Christian Nurture* (1861). Bushnell considered the spirit and character of parents to be the most important factors in the nurture of children, and the life of the family as the means whereby children learn to know and trust God. In addition to a theological and psychological discussion of the family as a means of Christian nurture, Bushnell provided practical suggestions for parent-child relationships, guidance on how to observe Sunday, information about the kind of religious instruction that is effective, and methods for family prayers.[24]

The Presbyterian church considered the family so important for the faith of parents and children that it offered a prize for the best book to encourage Christian family life. The winner, Joseph Collier, in his book *The Christian Home* (1859), first laid out a biblical and theological warrant for religion in the home and then instructed parents about their responsibility to provide for each other's spiritual welfare. In relation to children, Collier wrote, "God has thus appointed the parents to be the chief educators of the children, and has made the home the scene where, most of all, they are to be schooled in divine truth, and trained for his service." Collier continued with the following:

> The obligation to the *home instruction* of their children is laid upon every parent in the words, "Ye shall teach them to your children, speaking of them *when thou sittest in thine house.*" There are some who look upon the Sabbath-school as a substitute for the good old practice of our fathers in this respect. Never was there a greater mistake. It is indeed a beneficent institution, and a valuable *auxiliary* to fireside education, but it was never intended to supplant it. Let our children derive from it all the benefit they can, but let the parents also see to it that they receive at home, under his own eye and from his own lips, thorough, systematic instruction in Divinetruth.[25]

Bushnell, Collier, and others who wrote about family religion in the latter half of the 1800s were interested in what family religion could or should be. We do not have surveys of how families actually practiced their religion. Colleen McDannell, however, has collected information about families from 1840 to 1900, including their religious rituals. McDannell roots the family worship of evangelical Protestants in Puritan beliefs and practices. She writes, "Although the content of devotion would change during the nineteenth century, its structure remained the same. The family met in the morning and evening to recite prayers, sing psalms, and read from the Bible. Grace was said before and after meals . . . ."[26]

McDannell describes Victorian family religious practices in their material setting. This is important because the setting conveys feelings that may be as lasting as the worship. She notes the symbolic significance of Episcopalians having family prayers in the parlor before breakfast, whereas Methodist families did so in the dining room. She identifies the role of the father as the leader and provides pictures of families during prayers showing the position of children, servants, and pets. Of great importance was the large family Bible with marriage records and each child's birthday. The Bible was often placed on a table alone or with a hymnbook and candles that gave the appearance of a family altar.[27]

Sunday Schools

The story of the Sunday school in the 1800s, as written by Robert Lynn and Elliott Wright, helps us understand the evangelical enthusiasm underlying this movement, its widespread appeal, its growth, and its influence in a rapidly growing new nation in a new land. I need not repeat that history, for my purpose is to identify the role of the Sunday school in Protestants' education strategy.[28] The Sunday school was a successful agency of Christian education in the 1800s and served as an important part of church life for the following reasons.

First, for church people, the home was considered the place where children learned Christian faith and morals. The Sunday school, as Collier recorded in his book, was an auxiliary to home instruction. The Sunday school was a larger social setting where children could recite catechism questions and answers and Bible verses learned at home and where religious instruction was more systematic than home prayers.

Second, the religious practices and instruction in the public schools constituted a Bible-based Protestantism with a major emphasis on practical moral teachings. This was because Horace Mann and Henry Barnard, the first United States Commissioners of Education, did all they could to eliminate denominational doctrines from the public schools. These two influential leaders of the public school movement were religious, but they never tired of telling church leaders that the Sunday school was the place to teach various denominations' beliefs and practices. This the Sunday school could do well, for it was under the control of a congregation.

Third, the Sunday school was a practical form of evangelism that often led to the formation of a congregation. This evangelistic spirit was well illustrated by the American Sunday School Union in 1830 when it launched a drive "to establish a Sunday school in every destitute place where practical, through the valley of the Mississippi . . . ." At that time the valley covered two-thirds of the United States! The campaign was well financed and was led by laypeople who would start a Sunday school and then move on to another frontier settlement.[29] Years later Henry Barnard, looking back on the way the Sunday school movement started both common (public) schools and churches, wrote the following:

And in the less enlightened sections of our country, in many portions of the new States, and in many dark corners of our larger towns and cities, where vice and ignorance together congregate, the Sunday-school, by the self-denying labors of the missionary, with the aid of the even more unceasing and earnest philanthropist, the Sunday-school teacher, oftentimes becomes the precursor and pioneer both of the district school and of the church. In multitudes of instances it becomes both the moral and mental light of the neighborhood, and children and adults here learn to read who otherwise could not or would not do so.[30]

Fourth, the Sunday school was considered a social as well as a religious movement. This happened because its leaders were concerned about the welfare of children. For example, books, especially in rural areas, were scarce. The Sunday school movement began publishing inexpensive books, and it required its missionaries to start a library in every school they established so the public would have books of general interest. In 1859 the *Manual of Public Libraries* reported that of the more than 50,000 libraries in the United States, 30,000 were in Sunday schools.[31]

It is difficult for us today to realize that the Sunday school in the 1800s was considered an important way to help children become proper American citizens. This was demonstrated in conventions that, beginning in 1882, organized regional Sunday school unions and societies into a national movement. One convention, held in Washington, D.C., to raise money for the Mississippi Valley Campaign, was presided over by a senator, and the clerk of the House of Representatives was secretary. Seven senators spoke at the convention, including Daniel Webster and Francis Scott Key. The magnitude of the proposal appealed to the patriotism of these statesmen, and they commended it in the strongest terms as an important movement to promote the stability of the republic. The meeting was reported in the newspaper as "one of the most important ever held in the country."[32] This association of the Sunday school with social and political goals continued throughout the century. It probably reached its climax in 1910 when William Howard Taft, president of the United States, addressed the world's Sunday school convention. President Taft's speech included these words: "No matter what views are taken of general education, we all agree

. . . that Sunday school education is absolutely necessary to secure moral uplift and religious spirit."[33]

Social and business leaders who emerged after the Civil War also assumed responsibility for Sunday schools. John D. Rockefeller was superintendent of a Sunday school in Cleveland where his wife was a department head and his children often served as teachers. H. J. Heinz described himself as a man "who would rather be remembered as a Sunday school philanthropist than as the country's most successful pickle man." John Wanamaker, when postmaster general in Washington, D.C., always returned to Philadelphia on weekends to supervise a Sunday school.[34]

Higher Education

Protestants in the 1800s could depend on the ethos of society, the family, congregations, public schools, and the Sunday school to provide their children with Christian education. But going away to college meant leaving some of these influences behind. Protestants, therefore, founded colleges to extend their influence through higher education. Protestants were also motivated to maintain a Christian society by sponsoring higher education for lawyers, doctors, teachers, and business leaders. As a result of these motives, almost all colleges founded prior to the Civil War were established by churches. Needless to say, college graduates received and often accepted the Christian influence of the college they attended.[35]

THE 1800S PATTERN OF INFLUENCE

The following chart is a simplified way to illustrate how the ethos of a culture works through agencies to influence the life of a people. The chart does not assume that everybody in the 1800s was a Christian or lived by that lifestyle. Rather, the chart simply shows how the dominant interpretation of life was communicated to the rising generation. The solid lines indicate a direct pattern of influence. The broken line indicates some indirect influence.

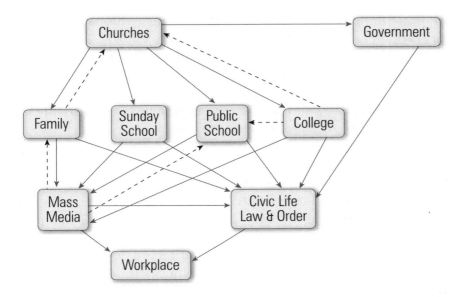

1900S: A TRANSFORMING ERA

What happened to this strategy throughout the 1900s? To answer that question it will not be necessary to trace the 100-year history of each of the above parts of the strategy. Rather, I will note what the situation is at the beginning of 2000s for each of the above agents of influence.

Ethos

The Protestant evangelical ethos that was so influential in the 1800s continued through the 1900s, but it encountered opposition from a liberal Protestant movement and from the growing secularization of American life in the second half of the 1900s.

It was not until the latter part of the 1800s, when American theological professors returned from study in Europe, that a liberal Protestantism began to flourish. During the early 1900s this liberal movement spread through most of the mainstream denominations. Evangelicals became defensive about their beliefs, which resulted in the formation of new denominations or contending interpretations of the Bible within denominations.[36] About mid-century, evangelicals began to obtain respect and influence. This came about through the leadership of Billy Graham and the quality of education offered by several evangelical seminaries, graduates of which enlarged the evangelical presence in mainstream Protestant denominations. Now, in the early years of the twenty-first century, evangelical Protestantism is increasing its presence and its influence in churches, reaching unchurched people through parachurch organizations, publishing interesting magazines and scholarly books, being very active in mission work worldwide, and expressing concern about certain social issues such as the right-to-life movement.

George Gallup is of the opinion that religion in general and Christianity in particular may become more important during the twenty-first century. He bases his opinion on surveys that show confidence in churches has remained steady for many years, belief in God is affirmed by about 95 percent of Americans, 92 percent of adults express a denominational preference, 69 percent of the people say they are members of a church or place of worship, and a majority of Americans say religion has an important place in their lives.[37]

One could link Gallup's opinion described above with the growth and influence of evangelicalism and conclude there may be a third great awakening in the early 2000s. I doubt that this will happen in the foreseeable future for several reasons.

One reason is that Gallup recognizes that religion today may be superficial. He cites three gaps. The first is the gap between what people say they believe and how they live. "While religion is highly popular in this country, survey evidence suggests that it does not change people's lives to the degree one would expect from the level of professed faith." A second gap is the one between "Americans' stated faith and their lack of the most basic knowledge about that faith." A third is the gap between people's beliefs and participation in a congregation. "Americans tend to view their faith as a matter between them and God, to be aided, but not necessarily influenced, by religious institutions." Stated in general terms, Gallup writes,

> We believe in God; but this God is often only an affirming one, not a demanding one, who does not command our total allegiance. We pray but often in a desultory fashion, with the emphasis on asking, or petition, not on thanksgiving, adoration, intercession, or forgiveness. We may revere the Bible, but many of us rarely read or study it. The proof is the sorry state of biblical knowledge among Americans—many are truly "biblical illiterates." Religious

ignorance extends to a lack of awareness and understanding of one's own religious traditions and of the central doctrines of one's faith. The result is that large numbers of Americans are unrooted in their faith and therefore, in the view of some, easy prey for movements of a far-ranging and bizarre nature. We pick and choose those beliefs and practices that are most comfortable and least demanding. Canadian sociologist Reginald Bibby calls this "religion a la carte."[38]

Perhaps Gallup's most disturbing statement about American religion at the beginning of 2000 was quoted from *The Saints Among Us.* This study concluded that "only 13% of Americans had what might be called a truly transforming faith, manifested in measurable attitudinal and behavioral ways."[39]

Another reason is that many of the leaders and all the adult population of the next generation—now children and youth—are being shaped by the secular spirit of our era. The number of people under the age of thirty with no religious affiliation is "steadily increasing as a proportion of the population and one likely to continue to do so."[40] This Gallup judgment that the number of people who profess no religion is increasing is supported by a study done at the Graduate Center of the City University of New York. This study "found that the number of adults who say they subscribe to no religion jumped from 14.3 million, or 8 percent of the total, in 1990 to 29.4 million, or 14 percent, in 2001."[41]

I believe that underlying the survey data quoted above is a spirit of secular individualism that has infected all of us and, through us, our congregations.[42] This spirit leads us to judge congregations on the basis of size, the splendor of their building, or the beauty of their worship services. Individuals select congregations that suit their convenience or provide the kind of membership that promises enjoyment without obligation. Ministers are selected for their ability to attract a crowd or for their pleasing personalities.

The vast array of evangelical churches is also infected with the spirit of secular individualism. Martin E. Marty, church historian, has written an analysis of how success and enormous wealth have changed evangelicalism. Evangelicals now use success (large numbers) to validate their beliefs. Among evangelicals, Sabbath observance is no longer unique, divorce is as common as among non-evangelicals, state-supported gambling to reduce taxes is not opposed, and rock music and other forms of entertainment are acceptable means to attract teenagers.[43]

The commercial success of blending secularism and individualism in a religious format is illustrated by "Roadhouse Revival," an Austin, Texas, radio program. It is aimed at "people who are comfortable both in the secular world and in the pew, those who admit that they like watching television, reading racy novels and drinking alcoholic beverages." This program is going nationwide because the creators have discovered it attracts mainstream as well as evangelical Christians with a variety of music including rock, blues, jazz, country, heavy metal, punk, and gospel. The creators of this program, who are also editors of *True Believers*, have discovered there is a vast audience in America that enjoys religion that does not require one to think or to change one's lifestyle.[44]

Cultural Values

Almost all the Gallup surveys in the 1990s noticed a huge gap between what people say about their religious beliefs and their lifestyle. As quoted above, Gallup judges that only 13 percent of Americans have a religious faith that orders their lifestyle. Since motivation for a person's actions is complex and changeable, I'm willing to assume that 13 percent may be too small. But even if we increase this percentage to 20 percent, this means that four out of every five Christians have their values formed by something other than their religion. I believe that the "something else" comes from our culture, which I have described as "secular individualism."

The word "secular" needs some interpretation. Secular knowledge in biology, geology, physics, and other hard sciences, plus the practical application of such knowledge, has greatly improved the quality and length of human life. I'm using the word "secular" to mean an orientation to the world as we know it in time and place rather than an orientation to God or to religious beliefs that transcend time and place. The word "individualism" also needs definition. Individuals make up culture; culture also makes up the individual's values. I'm using "individualism" to mean egoism—the notion that my interests, my comfort—in short, my life—is the basis for making judgments and decisions.

We see "secular individualism" clearly expressed in the way adults and teenagers prioritize their values according to one of Gallup's surveys.

> We want the fruits of faith, but less, its obligations. Of 19 social values, "following God's will" is far down the list among the public's choices as the "most important," behind happiness and satisfaction, a sense of accomplishment and five other values. Of eight important traits, teenagers rate "religious faith" as least important, behind patience, hard work, and five other traits.[45]

Robert Coles, Harvard University psychiatrist, directed the first study of children's beliefs and moral values. This study was of children in the fourth to the twelfth grades in public, private, and parochial schools located throughout the United States. Coles's summary of the study states that by age ten children have a "moral compass" by which they make moral judgments. Civic humanists (25 percent) are those who decide based on what is best for everybody. Conventionalists (20 percent) are those who decide what to do according to what is expected of them. Expressivists (18 percent) are those who make judgments on the basis of what makes them feel good. Theists (16 percent) are those who say they would do what God or their religion requires. Utilitarians (10 percent) make judgments on the basis of how it would serve their personal interests.[46]

The most recent national study of teenagers' religion was done by Christian Smith, a sociologist. His summary of data from teenagers about their understanding of and relation to God is as follows:

> . . . we suggest that the de facto dominant religion among contemporary U.S. teenagers is what we might call "Moralistic Therapeutic Deism." The creed of this religion, as codified from what emerged from our interviews, sounds something like this:
> 1. A God exists who created and orders the world and watches over human life on earth.
> 2. God wants people to be good, nice, and fair to each other, as taught in the Bible and by most world religions.
> 3. The central goal of life is to be happy and to feel good about oneself.

4. God does not need to be particularly involved in one's life except when God is needed to resolve a problem.
5. Good people go to heaven when they die.

Such a de facto creed is particularly evident among mainline Protestant and Catholic youth, but is also visible among black and conservative Protestants, Jewish teens, other religious types of teenagers, and even many non-religious teenagers in the United States.[47]

These studies of children's beliefs and moral values give us an indication of what the next adult generation will be like. We should not be surprised that the picture of these young people is remarkably similar to Gallup's data about adults of the 1990s. The Coles study found a huge gap between beliefs and lifestyle. When asked about belief in God, 82 percent affirmed that belief, but, as noted above, only 16 percent referred to God when making a moral judgment. Also, 39 percent of the children said they prayed, but only 2 percent would pray when they had to act in a particular moral situation. The researchers concluded, "This evidence raises the question of whether religion is becoming a sort of 'wallpaper factor'—stronger as a form of general background awareness than a truly decisive element in moment-by-moment decision making."[48]

It is always difficult to be precise about cultural values, but data from the above studies support Alan Wolfe's contention that individual rights have moved into the moral realm. He writes, "Now we live in an age of moral freedom, in which individuals are expected to determine for themselves what it means to lead a good and virtuous life . . . . The ultimate implication of the idea of moral freedom is not that people are created in the image of a higher authority. It is that any form of higher authority has to tailor its commandments to the needs of a real people."[49]

Public School and Religion

Our public schools at the beginning of the 1900s still had religious characteristics. Prayer and Bible reading started the day in most schools. *McGuffey's Readers* were used in some schools. Teachers reflected or did not openly challenge the cultural ethos.[50]

The religious character of public schools diminished rapidly in the early 1900s. Psychology and sociology, which developed in

Europe as a part of the Enlightenment, came to America at this time. These social sciences, plus John Dewey's philosophy of education, formed education into a field of research and study. Thus, education became a department in universities, and educators (not church leaders) gained control of the curriculum. Slowly, religion as a practice and Bible as a subject for study were eliminated or ignored. Through a series of Supreme Court cases ending in 1963, prayer, Bible reading, and teaching of the Bible in public schools have been ruled unconstitutional. Cases since 1963, such as the case of students leading a prayer before a football game (2000), have consistently followed the principle that public schools must be secular in every aspect. Religion can be taught "objectively," that is, as a secular subject, but few public schools elect to do so.

Congregations

Congregations continue to be the basic units of the Christian religion. Because congregations are at the center of this strategy, I will discuss their roles in Christian nurture in Part 2.

Previous comments about the way secular values influence congregations were illustrated by congregations concerned to get bigger, to be well regarded by the local newspaper, to have an imposing building with a fine worship service, and so on. I want to mention also that the sermon can be influenced by secular assumptions.

I do not want to overemphasize the role of the sermon in worship, for hymns, prayers, and Scripture all contribute to the worship of God. The sermon, however, is the formal presentation of beliefs and practices of Christianity to the congregation. Moreover, the sermon represents ministers' beliefs that will guide the way they lead the life and work of their congregations. So, it is important to review Marsha Witten's research at Princeton University as reported in *All Is Forgiven: The Secular Message in American Protestantism.*

Witten used the Southern Baptist denomination to represent evangelical churches and the Presbyterian Church (U.S.A.) to represent mainstream Protestantism. She requested 150 pastors of large churches in each denomination to send her a copy of a recent sermon preached on the parable of the prodigal son (Luke 15:11-32). She selected this passage because it would provide data about the preachers' images of God, their understandings of sin and salvation, their conceptions of how people relate to the world, and the nature of selfhood.

Modern Western culture affects religion, according to Witten's analysis, in three areas: it locates religion in one's private life, it assumes that religion is but one of many worldviews and lifestyles, and it provides rational ways of promoting and evaluating a church's program.

These three assumptions of secularity influenced the content of sermons in Presbyterian and Southern Baptist churches in a variety of ways. Concerning the first area, privatization, Witten wrote,

> Given the understanding of human selfhood that the language of psychology has contributed to contemporary religious speech, it is not surprising that God also is frequently characterized in terms of his internal states. We have seen God described in these sermons with respect to his thoughts, but even more so with respect to his feelings, particularly anguish and sorrow on behalf of his errant human children. Instead of rendering a transcendent God of majesty and power, many of the sermons depict God's psychological states and needs: the love he experiences for humankind in his role as daddy, the transparency of his longing for reunification with each individual person. If privatization has made it difficult for pastors to pose truth claims about objective realities—leaving only the realm of interior experience open to religious speech—it would seem reasonable that the God portrayed in the sermons would be configured by his subjectivity, just as human beings render and make sense of themselves.

Witten summarized some of her findings about the second area, pluralization, as follows:

> Consonant with contemporary marketing practices, religion (the "product") is posed as an answer to consumer needs; religious adherence is seen as solving problems that arise in the psychological or practical everyday experience of men and women. When we examine the "benefits" of religion offered in the sermons against the backdrop of contemporary culture, we can see the problems that the benefits are meant to address. To counter the cold, calculating weight of bureaucratic impartiality, the sermons offer self-esteem regardless of the merit one actually earns. In the context of a modern world that presupposes one's need for intimacy,

yet whose busyness and mobility make it difficult to attain, God is promised as a perfect interpersonal partner. In light of the uncertainties and complexities of contemporary pluralism, the speech holds forth the remission of anxiety and feelings of alienation. And as one's expressive side is dampened by the rationalization of modern work, the sermons teach people how to "get in touch" with their feelings.

Rationalization, the third area of secularization, is seen in the way many preachers standardize the procedure for conversion into steps that "are presented as the most straightforward, time-and-labor-saving path toward the given end." Human nature is also standardized so that the religious answer to human problems can be recommended to the largest number of people. This secular influence is also reflected in the way beliefs are used in sermons. Witten explains as follows:

> Akin to standardization of the self are other constructions in the speech which apparently are functional for the mass-marketing of religious adherence. Most obvious is the simplification of doctrine for mass consumption, as we have seen in the pastors' speech about God. First, as I pointed out, the Trinity—the precise configuration of whose nature was a matter of grave concern for theologians of the early church—has been collapsed in much of this speech into a single entity, an undifferentiated blend of the Persons. It is likely that this move has aided the tendency toward softening and mellowing God's transcendent characteristics, as the majestic remove of the Father gives way to the human qualities of the Son.

There is another way in which God's nature has been simplified in the speech of these sermons. Many of the sermons depict a God whose behavior is regular, patterned, and predictable; he is portrayed in terms of the consistency of his behavior, of the conformity of his actions to the single rule of "love." The listener always knows how God will act.

The above summary of Witten's research on the way secular assumptions have influenced Christian beliefs is not the whole story. She is careful to identify many Southern Baptists and some Presbyterians who resist these secular influences by preaching a more God-centered gospel and by relating what they say to biblical and timeless truths about human nature. Also, a few preachers went beyond accommodation or resistance to secularity as they suggested ways people could work through their religious dilemmas to find God's will for their lives.[51]

Sunday School

Protestants in the early 1900s continued to think of Sunday school as an important supplement to Christian education in the home, the public schools, congregational life, and the general influence of the community. As the public schools eliminated religion and society became more secular, churches responded in two ways. One way was to provide more agencies for Christian education, such as youth groups, vacation Bible schools, summer camps, conferences, and, after WWII, kindergartens and daycare centers. The other way to improve the educational work of the Sunday school was by providing curriculum based on secular educational psychology, urging teachers to take courses on teaching methods, and employing someone to direct the congregation's education program. Thus, by mid-century, Christian education, centered in the Sunday school, became a department of the congregation with its own director and, most often, with its own building modeled after public school buildings.

Mainstream Protestants, being middle class, by this time had accepted the idea that schooling was the way to learn whatever was wanted, be it dancing, acting, accounting, or subjects such as English or math. Then from mid-century on, as more women entered the workforce and as the time for family life together lessened, parents increasingly thought of the Sunday school as the place for children to learn their religion.

We, therefore, enter the 2000s with the idea that the Sunday school plus the add-ons—vacation Bible schools and maybe a summer youth camp—are adequate for the Christian education of our children. It is my contention that without a religious ethos, without support from public schools, and with little or no practice of religion in the family, the Sunday school plus the add-ons are seldom able to lead children into an understanding of God as their creator and redeemer. This reality is attributable to multiple causes.

The first cause, as discussed in the next two chapters, is that religion (or a faith in God) is formed in early childhood from children's relationships to their parents. Another cause is that Sunday school attendance for about thirty to forty minutes per week for about ten months a year is not time enough and not frequent enough to form beliefs and a lifestyle different from what the TV displays every day, from what the public schools explain about human life, and from the lifestyle parents model at home.

Family Life

We are all acquainted with the drastic changes in family life during the 1900s, so I will summarize them only briefly. Probably the most important change was from a broad consensus in the early 1900s that social values were practical principles derived from Christianity to what I have termed secular individualism. This change was well displayed in the data from Gallup's polls of the 1990s showing that adults judged happiness, satisfaction, a sense of accomplishment, and other values as being more important than seeking to know and follow God's will. The adults who were parents must have communicated those values to their children, for Gallup reported that teenagers put seven values ahead of religious faith. Moreover, the study supervised by Robert Coles reported that most children from ages ten to eighteen did not consider religion a decisive factor when making moral decisions.

The Presbyterian Church was singled out in the 1990s as a typical case of a denomination with a declining membership. One study, done by three sociologists, sought an answer to the question, "Why have so many young people departed from the church?" To answer this question they selected 500 young people who grew up in and were confirmed by the Presbyterian Church. Through telephone and face-to-face interviews they found that few of the proposed answers were given, such as the church is too liberal, too conservative, too institutional, or too remote from their concerns. Most of the young Presbyterians who lost interest in the church did so for what the researchers called "lay liberalism." It was "lay" because the young adults gave simple "homemade" reasons, and it was "liberal" because they considered Christianity a good religion but not the only true faith. Many of the respondents said that "they had only the vaguest idea what their own parents—or more commonly their father—believed, which suggests that silence on matters of faith is not new in many Presbyterian families."[52]

Secular individualism is not only modeled by parents in the home, but also it is communicated to children through the mass media, especially radio and TV, and through computers, which can produce an abundance of information and entertainment on demand. This entry of cultural values into the home is not new. Children in 1900 were exposed to some new ideas and differences in lifestyle by public school and by their reading. The differences were probably not great, but in any case parents were the authority figures that approved or disapproved whatever their children brought home. Today, secular values enter the home through mass media, entertainment, and technology-mediated information that children can command. Parents, therefore, face powerful competition from mass media partly because they can't control all the media-based messages their children receive and partly because their children will be influenced by friends whose parents do not object to secular values.

The struggle for the souls of children is complex today because cultural values are to some degree a part of their parents' lives. The 15 to 20 percent of adults and children who are trying to live by their faith in God also have to live in a culture that does not support that lifestyle.

Higher Education

Many of the colleges founded by churches in the 1800s continued in the 1900s. Church financial support for most of these colleges diminished during the past century so that by 2000 they had only a tenuous connection with a denomination. This happened because the colleges' needs for buildings, equipment, and well-prepared faculty cost more than the churches could supply. The colleges, then, sought funds from many sources, some of which did not care for or have an interest in religion. Also, many students who attended the colleges were more concerned about the colleges' ability to train them for a career than they were about its church affiliation. This does not mean that church colleges became as secular as state colleges or universities, but it does mean that Bible courses became optional or that a course in ethics, the psychology of religion, or philosophy could be substituted. Chapel worship was abandoned or made optional, and professors were selected solely on their competence in their field of study. This change in the nature of church-sponsored colleges plus the vast expansion of state institutions of higher education greatly reduced the church's influence in training professional leaders for society. This change also means that, with the exception of a few independent colleges or colleges still under the control of a denomination, the religious aspect of college education for Protestants today either consists of a few academic courses about religion or is ignored through an absence of religion altogether from their studies.

THE 2000S PATTERN OF INFLUENCE

Our current pattern of influence is difficult to display in a chart. The United States will soon have a population of 300 million people. It is a superpower in world affairs, and its scientific and medical achievements are outstanding. Religion and moral values continue to be a major characteristic of our society. Yet, as previously noted, a secular, individualistic, competitive spirit motivates most of the agents of our society and that spirit has, to some extent, penetrated our churches. The direct influence of our churches, except in issues such as same-sex marriage, abortion, or stem cell research, is rather weak. Churches have an indirect influence on our culture through the lives of individuals, but this is difficult to identify or display in a chart.

The chart that follows is my effort to identify the patterns of influence in our twenty-first-century culture. I suggest you change the chart better to reveal your ideas about how the spirit of our society is transmitted in the rising generation.

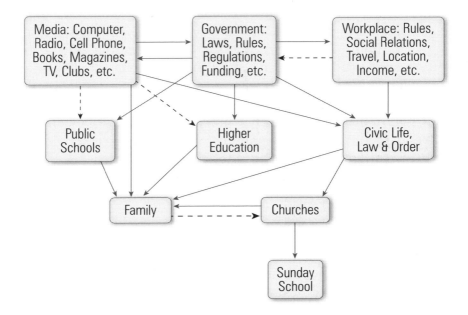

Notes

[1] Robert W. Lynn introduced me to the importance of "patterns of influence" for understanding the socialization process. See his *Protestant Strategies in Education* (New York: Association Press, 1964), 65. The following quote is from Robert Wuthnow, *Christianity and Civil Society* (Valley Forge PA: Trinity Press International, 1996), 26: "Oxford sociologist Bryan Wilson, a scholar who has spent a lifetime considering the question of secularization, has written that the best definition of it is not the decline of religion itself, but the decline in religion's ability to influence other spheres of life."

[2] R. Freeman Butts and Lawrence A. Cremin understood that culture as well as social institutions educate. See their *A History of Education in American Culture* (New York: Henry Holt and Co., 1953). Lawrence Cremin later defined education "as the deliberate, systematic, and sustained effort to transmit, evoke, or acquire knowledge, attitudes, values, skills or sensibilities, as well as any outcomes of that effort" (*Public Education* [New York: Basic Books, Inc., 1976], 7).

[3] Winthrop S. Hudson, *American Protestants* (Chicago: University of Chicago Press, 1961), 133.

[4] Ibid., 203.

[5] Winthrop S. Hudson, *Religion in America*, 2nd ed. (New York: Charles Scribner's Sons, 1973), 7-9, 76-82, 110, 131-57.

[6] Ibid., 141-44.

[7] Ibid., 228-34. Hudson, *American Protestants*, 123.

[8] Robert T. Handy, *A Christian America* (New York: Oxford University Press, 1971), vii. Although the social situation changed somewhat after the Civil War due to industrialization, urbanization, and vast immigration from Europe, Handy states that Protestants believed Christianity was the religion of civilization. See pp. 95-116.

[9] Handy, *A Christian America*, 27.

[10] Hudson, *American Protestantism*, 109-10.

[11] Martin E. Marty, *Protestantism in the United States: Righteous Empire*, 2nd ed. (New York: Charles Scribner's Sons, 1986), 67-97.

[12] Harriet Martineau, *Society in America*, ed. Seymour Martin Lipset (Garden City NJ: Doubleday & Co., Inc., 1962), 332-38.

[13] R. Freeman Butts, *A Cultural History of Education* (New York: McGraw-Hill Book Co., 1947), 487.

[14] Cited by John H. Westerhoff III, *McGuffey and His Readers* (Nashville: Abingdon Press, 1978), 15. For additional information about the *Readers*, see Mark Sullivan, *Our Times*, vol. 2 (New York: Charles Scribner's Sons, 1946), 7-48.

[15] Sullivan, *Our Times*, 2:89-90.

[16] Ibid., 15.

[17] Hudson, *American Protestants*, 110.

[18] Hudson, *Religion in America*, 129-30, 294.

[19] Rudy Ray Seward, *The American Family: A Demographic History* (Beverly Hills CA: Sage Publications, 1978), 12.

[20] Ibid., 26, 69.

[21] Alexis de Tocqueville, *Democracy in America*, ed. J. P. Mayer (Garden City NJ: Doubleday and Co., Inc., 1969), 290-91.

[22] Ibid., 590-95. See also his notes taken while visiting a frontier home in Appendix I, U, 731-33.

[23] Arthur W. Calhoun, *A Social History of the American Family*, vol. 2 (New York: Barnes and Noble, Inc., 1918), 138.

[24] Horace Bushnell, *Christian Nurture* (New Haven: Yale University Press, 1947).

[25] Joseph A. Collier, *The Christian Home* (Philadelphia: Presbyterian Board of Publication, 1859), 54.

[26] Colleen McDannell, *The Christian Home in Victorian America, 1840–1900* (Bloomington: Indiana University Press, 1986), 5.

[27] Ibid., 77-85. A fuller account of the role of the Bible in Victorian America, including photographs and drawings, will be found in Colleen McDannell, *Material Christianity* (New Haven: Yale University Press, 1995), 67-99. The religious life of families also included the use of books with readings similar to those in *McGuffey's Readers*. One that I examined was published in England and used by Methodists in the United States with "little children." For each month of 1847, there is a chapter containing Bible stories, poems, stories with a moral or about historical figures, Proverbs, and the like. The selections were to be read to or by a child. See *Early Day of the Wesleyan Scholars Guide*, vol. 2 (London: James Mason, 1847).

[28] Robert W. Lynn and Elliott Wright, *The Big Little School* (New York: Harper and Row, 1971). For an account of how the Sunday school became a part of the church's strategy of Christian education, see William B. Kennedy, *The Shaping of Protestant Education*, ed. C. Ellis Nelson (New York: Association Press, 1966).

[29] Ibid., 17-32.

[30] Quoted by Kennedy, *Shaping of Protestant Education*, 21.

[31] Lynn and Wright, *Big Little School*, 31.

[32] Clarence H. Benson, *History of Christian Education* (Chicago: Moody Press, 1943), 158.

[33] William Howard Taft, "The President's Estimate of the Sunday-school," *World-wide Sunday-school Work*, ed. William N. Hartshorne (Chicago: Executive Committee of the World's Sunday School Association, 1910), 125.

[34] Lynn and Wright, *Big Little School*, 71.

[35] Donald G. Tewksbury, *The Founding of American Colleges and Universities Before the Civil War* (North Haven CT: Archon Books, 1965), 55-132.

[36] John Seel, *The Evangelical Forfeit* (Grand Rapids: Baker Books, 1993).

[37] George H. Gallup, Jr., *Religion in America* (Princeton: Princeton Religion Research Center, 1996), 16-17.

[38] Ibid., 8-9.

[39] Ibid., 14.

[40] George H. Gallup, Jr., and Jim Castelli, *The People's Religion* (New York: MacMillan Publishing Co., 1989), 264.

[41] Carol Eisenberg, "Number of Americans professing no religious faith doubles during the 90s," *Austin American-Statesman*, 6 November 2001, E6.

[42] For a fuller discussion of "secular individualism" see C. Ellis Nelson, *How Faith Matures* (Louisville: Westminster/John Knox Press, 1989), 21-42.

[43] Martin E. Marty, "Will Success Spoil Evangelicalism?" *Christian Century* 117/21 (19-26 July 2000): 757-61.

[44] Kim Sue Lia Perkes, "Praise the Lord and turn up the radio," *Austin American-Statesman*, 29 July 2000, A1. For a brief overview of the many expressions of contemporary evangelicalism see Gallup and Castelli, *The People's Religion*, 92-98.

[45] Gallup, *Religion in America*, 9.

[46] Robert Coles, Project Director, *Girl Scouts Survey on the Beliefs and Moral Values of America's Children* (New York: Girl Scouts of the United States of America, 1989), xiv.

[47] Christian Smith, *Soul Searching: The Religious and Spiritual Lives of American Teenagers* (New York: Oxford Press, 2005), 162-63.

[48] Coles, *Girl Scouts Survey*, 23.

[49] Alan Wolfe, "The Final Freedom," *The New York Times Magazine*, 18 March 2001. For a fuller description of secularism and its influence on church life see my *How Faith Matures* (Louisville: Westminster/John Knox Press, 1989), 19-61.

[50] Charles R. Kniker, "New Attitudes and New Curricula: The Changing Role of the Bible in Protestant Education, 1880–1920," *The Bible in American Education*, ed. David L. Barr and Nicholas Piediscalzi (Philadelphia: Fortress Press, 1982), 121-43.

[51] Marsha G. Witten, *All Is Forgiven: The Secular Message in American Protestantism* (Princeton: Princeton University Press, 1993), 129-40.

[52] Benton Johnson, Dean R. Hoge, and Donald Luidens, "Mainline Churches: The Real Reason for Decline," *First Things* 31 (March 1993): 13-18.

Chapter 2

PARENTS:

THE PRIMARY SOURCE FOR CHILDREN'S IMAGES OF GOD

Pastors, Christian educators, and church leaders have known for some time that American culture has changed as described in the previous chapter. Their response has been to improve the schooling model of nurture, such as providing better curriculum for the Sunday school, training ministers for youth groups, and encouraging adult Bible study classes. These efforts to improve instruction have been helpful, but they do not adequately challenge the powerful influence of our secular society. There is probably not much more that can be done as long as we start with the question, "How and what should we teach to each age group in the church?"

We need to change the question to, "How do children learn about God?" This question comes at a time when we have considerable research on how children learn and some data on the specific matter of learning about God.

In this chapter I will review research on how children by the age of three have primitive mental images of God, based on their relation to their parents. In the next chapter I will present cases to show how children as they grow relate their idea of God to the experiences they are having.

PERSONAL RELIGION

Religion is first personal and it remains personal throughout one's life. The issue we must resolve is not the personal aspect of a person's religious faith; rather, the issue is, as the Apostle Paul wrote, whether we can put away our childish understanding of God in order to become mature in our relationship with God (1 Cor 13:11-13; Eph 4:11-16). We will not be able to make this move toward spiritual maturity unless we understand that in the deepest levels of our being there may be ideas of God that need correction.

It is difficult, however, to change our images of God because these images were first formed out of childish wishes. An example of individualistic religion was recorded by Robert Bellah and associates in their study of values by which Americans live. Sheila Larson, a young nurse, described her faith as "Sheilaism." "I believe in God. I'm not a religious fanatic. I can't remember the last time I went to church. My faith has carried me a long way. It's Sheilaism. Just my own little voice."[1]

From a psychological perspective, Sheila has an adult version of an infant's religion. It is personal. It is self-centered. It satisfies her and requires little obligation to act in any way other than to please herself. Sheila formed her conception of religion as a child, but she never attempted to reform it as she grew in experience and in the ability to think about God.

We should not criticize Sheila too harshly. She formed her first beliefs about God in her childhood. So do we. What is important is for us to gain an understanding of how our childhood experiences shaped our primal images of God. By doing so we can begin the process of giving up or transforming that early image of God.

Notice that I have shifted from religion to a mental image of God. A person's image of God is more important than that person's religion. Religion can mean many things. It can refer to personal lifestyle, to one's beliefs, to church membership, to being a member of a religious order or cult, or to something as vague as an inner feeling of dependence on a higher power. Underneath each of these expressions of religion is an image of what God is like and what God expects.

The difference between religious beliefs and church members' images of God can be seen in almost any congregation. Although all members of a congregation may have the same theology, there will probably be differences on ethical issues and policies regarding use of property, service to the community, and similar matters. Take abortion as an example. Some church members may have mental images of God that absolutize the beginning of human life at conception, so they are "pro-life." Others in the same congregation think of God as one who allows several factors to influence a decision about abortion, so they are "pro-choice." Likewise, underneath beliefs about war, uses of natural resources, homosexual relations, or other ethical issues are a person's deeply rooted sentiments or images of God.

Personality or character traits also affect a person's practice of religion. Some Christians, although professing forgiveness and love as the major beliefs in their religion, are vindictive and unforgiving toward people they do not like. Contrariwise, it is not uncommon to see people who claim no religious beliefs, yet who display kind and forgiving character traits.

It is rather obvious, therefore, that psychological factors such as feelings, affections, and attitudes formed in early childhood shape our images of God. This highly personalized God is, psychologically speaking, expressed in whatever religion or lifestyle we adopt.

COMPOSING A SELF

Why do infants during their first three years of life form images of God? The answer is that infants are learning to compose a self as they respond to caregivers and the conditions in which they find themselves. After about three years of such responding, they have a primitive answer to the fundamental questions about God, death, and behavior.

Since our concept of the self is subjective, all efforts to account for its origin, development, and function are tentative. It is almost impossible for older children or adults to recall events or feelings during the first two years of life. In the past, therefore, researchers waited until children had good use of language before studying their sense of themselves. In recent decades, however, researchers have developed techniques to study infants and have compiled an enormous amount of data about the way a typical infant acquires a sense of self.

Psychologists who specialize in child development publish a handbook about every fifteen years to record their latest research data and theories. The fifth edition, dated 1998, consists of four volumes of more than one thousand pages each.[2] Many articles start with a sentence such as, "There has been an explosion of research during the past twenty years," or "Since the last edition of this handbook there has been an enormous advance in our knowledge of early childhood." The reason for these extravagant appraisals is the way new technology has been used to gain access to infants' mental and emotional development. For example, video cameras set up to continuously record the interaction of caregivers with infants provide accurate data about the way infants respond to people in their homes and daycare centers.

Neuroscientists, such as John T. Bruer, have learned a lot about the brain's development during the first three years of life. But what they have learned does not have a practical effect on the way an infant forms a self. Also, brain scientists do not offer any practical advice on how to raise a child other than the following common-sense guidance: "Be attentive to the baby; read, sing, and talk to the baby; be selective about television; choose day care that provides safe, attentive care for your child."

What neuroscientists have to offer, according to Bruer, is an understanding that the brain is so plastic that it responds throughout life to what the mind, including one's attitudes and values, requires of it. Although the brain as a biological organ develops rapidly in early childhood, children's selves are formed by the culture in which they live and the particular conditions to which they must respond.[3]

The receptivity of babies' brains to culture is illustrated in their acquisition of language. Katherine Long's report on what is known from the new methods of brain science states that "an explosion of growth occurs in the first three years of life. At birth, a baby's brain contains about 100 million neurons, the brain cells that carry electrical messages through the brain. Each one can produce up to 15,000 synapses, or connections to other brain cells. These synapses are the key to healthy development and learning." Biologically speaking, when the synapses are activated and exercised they tend to become permanent. Thus, when parents talk to their baby, they are helping to "wire" the infant's brain for language. Long's report includes a statement from Patricia Kuhl, who has done research on when babies learn language. She has concluded, "There isn't a single speech sound contrast used in the world's languages that infants can't distinguish at birth." According to Kuhl, infants have learned sounds that are distinctive within their native language by the age of six months. By eleven months babies start to lose the ability to differentiate between phonetic sounds that are not in their native language.[4]

The plasticity of babies' brains is illustrated in what has been learned from Romanian orphans. For some time students of child development—medical doctors, psychologists, educators, and psychiatrists—have warned that the absence of caregivers who lovingly handle, play with, and talk to a baby can cause serious behavioral problems. Babies who grew up under these adverse conditions were observed to be withdrawn, apathetic, and, perhaps, slow learners. Although researchers have been unable to test this notion because they could not subject human babies to adverse living conditions, in the early 1990s an unprecedented opportunity to study the effects of early deprivation of infants occurred. This came about because the dictator of Romania, Nicolae Ceausescu, had been encouraging women to have babies and turn them over to the state orphanages to be trained. The orphans were fed, clothed, and kept in beds, but given little attention. After the Communist regime was overthrown in 1989, the orphans were allowed to be adopted. About 10,000 of these children have been adopted by citizens in the United States. The *U.S. News & World Report* summarized the situation as follows:

> Nearly every child brought out of Romania at first bore telltale deficits from lack of stimulation: in speech, in relating to others, and sometimes even in being able to chew solid food.
>
> The only thing more remarkable than the damage caused by neglect, say researchers now charting the Romanian adoptees, is many children's ability to overcome the setbacks once the neglect ended. Case Western Reserve University professor of social work Victor Groza has been following more than 300 Romanian adoptees since 1992 and has found that 80 percent of the children have already made up quite well for lost time. After the first year, says Groza, 20 percent of adoptees had adapted so well that it was all but impossible for him to distinguish them from typical children their age. An additional 60 percent showed subtle problems like slower eye-hand coordination. In the 20 percent who fared worst, Groza found more intractable cognitive, behavioral, and

emotional problems, such as severe temper tantrums. Researchers in Britain and Canada have come up with similar results.

As a general rule, the longer the stay in an orphanage, the more severe the problems and the longer it takes for the children to recover. In fact, it's commonly assumed that neglected children adopted after age 2 are irreversibly damaged. But the brain is so adaptable that no child should be branded a lost cause, says Harvard neuroscientist Mary Carlson. Even though it seems easiest for children to master tasks such as speaking or reading during certain periods, it almost never becomes impossible.[5]

One child, adopted by Denise Sobleski, was named Nicky. At seven months Nicky weighed fifteen pounds, was "covered in sores, and couldn't move his atrophied little muscles." Denise enrolled him in a special gym program at eighteen months in order to help him walk and at the age of three enrolled him in a preschool program to prepare him for kindergarten. With these and other efforts to help Nicky, he is now, at age nine, reading at high school level and learning to play the piano.

THINKING

Just as infants have the ability to distinguish differences in speech sounds after birth, they have the ability to think. It is difficult for adults to realize that infants think because adults assume that thinking means analyzing situations rationally. Infants are not rational, for their brains are not fully developed, they do not have a fund of information, and they have little memory. But if we define thinking as "goal-directed cognitive activity," then infants learn how to think soon after birth.[6]

At three months of age infants have learned that objects fall when released. At four months they understand that objects exist even if put out of sight. At six months infants manipulate objects according to their purpose. At one year of age infants look for causes behind what happens and they are on their way to a problem-solving method of thinking that is well established by eighteen months of age. At two years of age, when infants can talk fairly well, their ability to observe and to think becomes more obvious. By three years of age infants have worked out a naive understanding of physics, psychology, and biology.[7]

Some researchers believe that children, especially after two years of age, do more active thinking than adults. This is because children are amazed at all the things going on about them, are required to solve many practical problems, and are open to a discussion of how things work.[8]

For example, Tristan at three years of age asked, "Why doesn't my blood come out when I open my mouth?" Antonine at the same age watched his mother futilely trying to retrieve a helium-filled balloon that had lodged underneath a high-ceilinged stairwell. He said, "Mother, just make it go over to the side and you can walk upstairs and get it."[9]

BECOMING SELF-CONSCIOUS

Just as infants' thinking grows from vague efforts to get what they want to simple problem-solving in three years, so does self-consciousness. Infants grow from making unconscious responses to caregivers to conscious accounts of themselves as a person. A consensus of research data about infants' development of selfhood can be gleaned from Susan Harter's research.

From birth to four months one can see an emerging organization as babies adjust to a schedule of sleeping, feeding, elimination, and handling by caregivers.

From four to ten months there is increasing differentiation from caregivers. This comes about during the rituals of feeding, dressing, bathing, and play. Researchers have noted that during this period babies begin to learn that they can do things such as make a mobile move. As they respond to games like peek-a-boo or tickling followed by "I'm going to get you," infants begin to learn that they are separate persons, yet bonded to their caregivers.

During the time from ten to fifteen months there are many experiences infants share with caregivers. As a result infants begin to understand that they have minds of their own. Infants pay close attention to caregivers and communicate through body language and vocal noise. They know, for example, how to ask for a cookie or how to turn away from someone who is trying to get them to do something they don't want to do.

After fifteen months the growth of self-understanding increases rapidly. By eighteen months infants recognize themselves in a mirror. They become more self-assertive. They develop ideas of what they want to do independently of caregivers. Some infants at this age have worked out strategies to get their parents to give them what they want.

At two years of age infants are rather independent and are on their own for longer periods of time. They are learning to coordinate their wishes with those of caregiving adults. They are also able to get by with behavior they know is not approved.

The great leap forward is between the second and third birthdays. Because infants during this time become more talkative, they ask questions and engage in conversations that enhance their self-consciousness. With better command of language, infants begin their life stories. They identify themselves to others, tell what has happened to them, or explain how they feel. They now know themselves as persons with attributes, interests, and thoughts that are theirs.[10]

An illustration of growing self-consciousness from my own life involves our son Stark, who as an infant had vivid red hair. When he was introduced to people, they always asked the same questions in the same order. He soon got tired of the same set of questions, so he worked out a response when introduced to a person. He would say, "My name is Stark. I'm three years old. I don't know where I got it."

PRIMAL IMAGES OF GOD

This brief outline of infants' development of thinking and of growing consciousness of self will not surprise parents who pay attention to the development of their children. What parents may not understand is that during these same years infants form their first images of God. They do so because, as the ability to think expands, they wonder about the world they are discovering. Let's first note a psychological description of infants' innate desire to create as a part of their self-consciousness and then note how an initial image of God emerges.

Innate Desire to Create

One school of child development psychologists thinks in terms of three areas of the self. One is the inner self as it evolves according to the above outline. Another is the external world that impinges on the infant through the relationship to caregivers and circumstances (food, shelter, medical treatment, and cultural environment) in which the infant/mother live. The third area of reality is termed "transitional phenomena."

The transitional phenomena begin to appear during the period from four to ten months. Before this time, infants accept food and handling by mothers as experiences infants create to satisfy their needs; now infants begin to realize mothers and things are separate and there are limits to what infants can do or expect. W. D. Winnicott, a practicing pediatrician as well as a psychoanalyst, noted that babies, in addition to thumb-sucking, would with the other hand take part of the sheet into the mouth, would hold an object close at hand, would pluck threads from clothing or blankets, or would start to use babbling sounds or special noises. Winnicott describes how we may observe the way infants are starting to create a reality between inner and outer demands.

> Also, out of all this (if we study any one infant) there may emerge some thing or some phenomenon—perhaps a bundle of wool or the corner of a blanket or eiderdown, or a word or tune, or a mannerism—that becomes vitally important to the infant for use at the time of going to sleep, and is a defense against anxiety, especially anxiety of depressive type. Perhaps some soft object or other type of object has been found and used by the infant, and this then becomes what I am calling a *transitional object*. This object goes on being important. The parents get to know its value and carry it around when traveling. The mother lets it get dirty and even smelly, knowing that by washing it she introduces a break in continuity in the infant's experience, a break that may destroy the meaning and value of the object to the infant.[11]

The term "transitional object" may convey a false impression. The word "transitional" does not mean a temporary way station between two developments of the self. The term is used to describe the way an infant creates a reality between inner and outer reality. Although this created reality relates to inner and outer experience, it is a separate reality. It is the earliest experience of an infant having control over an object and of the caregiver's respect for what the infant is creating. Normally, however, children lose interest in the objects of infancy as they acquire new and different objects.

Moreover, the "transitional" reality continues throughout life as individuals must continue to relate inner needs and interests to the requirements of living with other people.

The word "object" calls attention to the thing the infant has used to create a reality different from inner or outer experience. To Winnicott, however, what is important is the natural way this phenomenon occurs between infants and caregivers. Parents accept a blanket or teddy bear as something the infant cares about and allows the infant control over the object. Winnicott terms this an "intermediate area . . . that is allowed to the infant between primary creativity and objective perception based on reality-testing."[12] Once this process begins, it "widens out into that of play, and of artistic creativity and appreciation, and of religious feeling, and of dreaming, and also of fetishism, lying and stealing, the origin and loss of affectionate feeling, drug addiction, the talisman of obsessional rituals, etc."[13]

Play is the activity that introduces that transitional reality between self and others. Play can be observed as early as the period between two and six months. Caregivers play "peek-a-boo," "I'm gonna get you," or similar games that cause the infant excitement and delight. This play activity requires a caregiver, so a self/other dialectic creates the transitional reality. When babies are old enough to build a tower with blocks, they often knock it down. Building the tower was play; it was a creation of the self. After the tower stood for a few minutes, the child began to see it as a physical object outside the child's control. By knocking it down the child enhances the self's authority to do what it wants to do.

Transitional objects that infants create out of a blanket or a toy are indications of what they are using to form a self. The physical objects thus used will be abandoned as others take their place. But the most important objects being formed within infants are images of persons, especially the caregivers, and the quality of an infant's bonding with caregivers will be affective throughout the infant's life.

Mental Image

Perhaps it would be helpful if we shift from our discussion of transitional objects to the term of "mental image" since our interest is in the image formed in the mind as a result of a relationship to others.

We internalize an image of a person in terms of our experience with that person. Our mental image of a person may be vague, but we constantly revise it as we get to know that person better. Whatever image we have, be it that the person is thoughtful but timid, thoughtful but aggressive, well-intended, deceitful, thrifty, loyal, or a combination of many characteristics, that mental image will guide all we say and do when we are with that person.[14]

Years ago I was with a small group engaged in a conversation about Joe, a college president whom all but one of us knew. We talked of various things Joe had done that impressed us concerning his administrative ability. When we were about to move to another topic, the woman who did not know Joe asked, "But what kind of person is he?" My silent reaction was, hasn't she been listening? Didn't she understand what we said about Joe's excellent record as a college president? In recalling that event recently I have come to believe that woman's question is the most important question we can ask about a person. She was indicating that achievement alone did not provide her with enough information to form a good mental image of Joe as a person. She wanted to know how Joe treated people, how he used his time and money, what he cared about other than his position, and other matters related to Joe as a human being.

Having a mental image of another person does not mean our image of a person corresponds to who the person actually is. This situation is caused in part because we know a person only in the relationship we have had with the person and what that person has selected to reveal. It is caused in part because we form our image of a person out of our special psychological needs, which may not be based on who the person really is. Thus, the images we have of other people are real in our minds and may endure despite evidence to the contrary. Those images influence our perceptions, beliefs, and behavior.

"Mental images" is also the term for our explanation of how God is represented in a person's mind. "Image" does not mean a photograph, although children can translate their images of God into a drawing if requested. A mental image includes a set of feelings—the source of which may be partly unconscious—that one uses to describe a person or an entity one has created in the mind. It is for this reason that an image of God is more significant for religion than a vague statement of one's outlook such as "faith." For example, Erik Erikson identifies the psychosocial developmental goal for the first year of life as the acquisition of "basic trust."[15] By using a functional interpretation of religion, Erikson is able to point out that basic trust has "the capacity for faith—a vital need for which man must find some institutional confirmation."[16] Erikson notes that individuals may find institutions other than religious ones in which their need for faith might be fulfilled. "Basic trust" may lead to faith in God, but it does not provide us with an image of God.

An image of God is a precise and dynamic element within the self. It is the reality within one's being with which one carries on a conversation. Moreover, one can have an image of God of which one is afraid or which one does not like. Atheists have images of God in which they do not believe.[17] So, for our purpose, we will separate the mental image of God from the general feeling of "basic trust."

Primal God Representation

An image of God is created by infants by the end of their third year. This earliest image of God is formed to satisfy the psychological needs in their self-formation, and it reflects their experience with caregivers. According to Anne-Maria Rizzuto, the process starts at birth because the parents' interpretation of the birth influences their response to the infant. The parents' desire for the baby, their understanding of their role in caring for the baby, their financial, social, and educational status, and other such factors are influential in their relationship to the child. Religious parents will probably have a baptism or dedication service symbolizing their understanding of God. The particular way the mother starts the self-development of the infant is through eye contact and reflecting back to the child a sense of the child's status. In a healthy relationship the infant absorbs a feeling of being loved and wanted.[18]

During the first seven or eight months the infant has experiences of a physical nature related to caregivers such as being fed, bathed, held; looking at the parent's face; and hearing sounds and music. Experiences of this type continue throughout infancy and are preserved as eidetic memories. They may be later linked to a particular God image and may result in a good feeling when singing "Safe in the Arms of Jesus," "O Love that Will Not Let Me Go," "God Will Take Care of You," "Jesus, Lover of My Soul, Let Me to Thy Bosom Fly," or the refrain "And I shall see Him face to face." These early experiences form a feeling based on which a particular God image may be built. These experiences of infancy continue into childhood and are preserved, often unconsciously in the self, regardless of the stage of cognitive development. Later, when individuals develop the ability to reason abstractly, there may be an effort to bring these early feeling states into harmony with reason, but this is difficult to accomplish.

Infants' use of transitional objects during the time from about seven to fifteen months indicates that they are becoming more self-conscious. Moreover, their relationship with caregivers becomes more intense as they assert the self that is forming. Self-formation results from the self-consciousness that is being evoked by the care-givers and the memories of experiences the infant has had with the caregivers. These two activities, going on simultaneously, are defining the personality of the infant. Incidentally, this *process* of forming a self continues throughout one's life, as one must relate one's self to the inner representation of persons with whom one relates in social or business affairs.

During this period when the infant is developing a sense of self as distinct from other people, there is no conscious God representation. The interaction of the infant with parents, however, is creating the sentiments (emotionally charged attitudes or dispositions) from which a God representation will emerge.

During or toward the last half of the third year infants develop images of God that they can describe. These images will become more clearly focused at they grow. But even by age four children can indicate the characteristics of their God by drawing or dictating a letter to God.[19]

The God images infants create between their second and third birthdays differ from other objects they internalize. The God image is not static. It is an inner feeling that influences their ideas of the world and their behavior. This does not mean that the God image is something they like. Some infants dislike or are indifferent to their God image. A child as young as five may—because of the death of the father—blame God and decide not to respect God.[20] Like conscience, with which the God image may become fused in a year or two, the God image is an inner reality the child cannot ignore. It is the only reality within the self that knows all about the self and is related to all the problems and feelings of the self.

The God image is also unique among the objects represented in the infant's self because it endures throughout the life span. This comes about because most parents—and society generally—reinforce the God image and negate other images. Although the God image is created at a time when the infant may internalize a mental image of ghosts, monsters, witches, or Santa Claus, these latter images are slowly suppressed by caregivers and society. The God image is encouraged or is allowed to be whatever the infant says it is, on the theory the infant will "outgrow" the primitive image of God. One does not, however, outgrow the primitive image of God. Rather, the reality of that image within the self has to be reconciled with ongoing experiences. Some people are able to give up childish ways in religion, as the Apostle Paul urged them to do, so that they would be able to reason like an adult (1 Cor 13:11). But many people are not able to overcome fear, loneliness, or lack of self-confidence characterizing their private God image without the help of psychotherapy.[21]

The primitive image of God that is in place at about the age of three is unique for each person. It is a personal God constructed out of material from two sources. The first source is the internalized image and feeling states from relations with parents, siblings, and playmates; the second is the social, economic, and religious situation in which the family lives.[22] The second includes the instructions caregivers have given the child. The child at age three is conscious of cause-and-effect relationships and wants to know what caused the wind to blow, the pet dog to die, or the sun to rise each morning. If caregivers explain that God is connected to these events, then that cause will probably be accepted as part of the child's God image. The child could also be told that "these things just happen" or that "later you will understand." In any case, children will collect bits and pieces of what they are told in order to construct a God image.

Once the child has formed an image of God within the privacy of the mind, that image has the role of a person who has been internalized.[23] The God image has a somewhat independent status. The dialogue and the emotional relationship between the God image and the self is like that which exists between two persons. The relation can be friendly, supportive, judgmental, forgiving, suggestive as to how to act, or some combination of the above, depending on the circumstances the self is facing. The self can also resist, reject, or deny any relation to the God image.

An illustration of how children toward the end of their third year form a God image came in a letter from a friend. Our friend, Ruth, is the mother of Kristin, age two years and eleven months. The letter reads, "Kristin and I had our first heavy philosophical discussion Sunday night as we were leaving the grocery store. She said, 'I like your green car, Mom.' I said, 'Thanks. It belonged to Grandpa Brice.' She said, 'He's dead, isn't he?' I said, 'That's right.' She said, 'He's in heaven with God.' I said, 'Good for you, sweetheart!' Then she said, 'He's in God's tummy.'" Kristin has already formed and answered, with the help of her God image, a profound question: Where do people come from and where do they go?

By the time children are five or six years old they have settled into patterns of response to parents and other people; have formed likes and dislikes for clothes, food, and events; have experienced the death of bugs or pets; have seen a vast array of life situations on TV; have begun to read, tell time, and participate in making plans for family activities. All of these achievements contribute to their clearer image of God and to their understanding of reasons for that image. Helen Carboon, wanting to know what children thought about God as they entered their first year of school and desiring to help parents understand their role in forming faith in God, studied more than 500 Catholic children aged five or six. Her study, based on children's explanations of their drawings of God, provides us with many examples of how children incorporate ideas about God from church teachings, religious practices in the home, life experiences, and imagination. The main source for their image of God, however, was their relationship to their parents. Carboon explains why children's relation to parents is the major source of their idea of God in the following statement.

> Parents are undoubtedly the most important "God-bearers" for children, not so much in what they say, but in who they are for their sons and daughters. Imagine a parent from a child's perspective: this physically big person, who is strong and capable, able to

lift and carry the child, able to do so much that is beyond the child's capabilities. This big person who has seemingly all power over the child, this person who makes decisions and gives directions, who provides or does not provide what the child needs for his/her physical well-being. This big person who can reward and punish, who can give and receive love, affection, approval or disapproval. This big and powerful person who reflects back to the child who the child is, accepting or rejecting the child in this same reflection. Initially the parent is God for the child, so it is not at all surprising that the child uses his/her parent or parents in forming his/her image of and relationship with his/her God. The importance of parents was expressed, usually quite simply, but sometimes with some telling elaboration:

"Mum and Dad remind me of God because they say nice things to me."
"When I look at Mummy I think of God."
"My Dad reminds me of God. He looks like him."
"Mum and Dad remind me of God because maybe they look a bit like what maybe God looks like."[24]

This chapter has been a psychological description of how infants form an initial image of God. The purpose was to show that our deep convictions about the nature of God are rooted in our early childhood experiences, especially with our caregivers. The result of this rootage is a highly personal idea of God that underlies any religious organization to which we may belong or any lifestyle we favor.

NOTES

[1] Robert N. Bellah et al., *Habits of the Heart* (Berkeley: University of California Press, 1985), 221.

[2] William Damon, ed., *Handbook of Child Psychology*, 5th ed. (New York: John Wiley & Sons, 1998).

[3] John T. Bruer, *The Myth of the First Three Years* (New York: Free Press, 1999). The entire book is helpful in sorting out what is known about the brain in relation to widely held assumptions about the importance of the first three years. The reference cited in the first paragraph about neuroscientists is on pages 183-88. The reference for the second paragraph about neuroscientists is from pages 181-210. There are many references throughout the book illustrating the plastic nature of the brain—for example, on the power of culture, pages 53-54; on the critical period for learning, pages 128-43; and on what kind of interventions are effective, pages 159-74.

[4] Katherine Long, "Baby's brain begins distinguishing life experiences very early," *Austin American-Statesman*, 4 July 1997, E4.

[5] Joannie Schrof Fischer, "From Romania, a lesson in resilience," *U.S. News & World Report*, 13 September 1999, 50.

[6] Judy S. Deloache, Kevin F. Miller, and Sophia L. Pierroutsakos, "Reasoning and Problem Solving," in *Handbook of Child Psychology*, 2:803. All of volume 2 is about "cognition, perception, and language." The chapters on "Infant Cognition," "Representation," "Language Acquisition," "Knowledge Acquisition in Foundation Domains," and "Social Cognition" are of special value for understanding how infants' minds develop.

[7] Henry M. Wellman and Susan A. Gelman, "Knowledge Acquisition in Foundational Domains," in *Handbook of Child Psychology*, 2:554-63. See also chapter 14, "Cognition as a Collaborative Process."

[8] Deloache et al., "Reasoning and Problem Solving," 2:802.

[9] Ibid., 801-802.

[10] Susan Harter, "The Development of Self-Representations," in *Handbook of Child Psychology*, 3:553-600. See also Daniel N. Stern, *The Interpersonal World of the Infant* (New York: Basic Books, 1985).

[11] D. W. Winnicott, *Playing and Reality* (London: Tavistock Publications, 1971), 4.

[12] Winnicott, *Playing and Reality*, 11.

[13] Ibid., 5.

[14] J. R. Greenberg and S. A. Mitchell, *Object Relations in Psychoanalytic Theory* (Cambridge: Harvard University Press, 1983), 9-12.

[15] E. H. Erikson, *Insight and Responsibility* (New York: W. W. Norton, 1964), 69.

[16] E. H. Erikson, *Identity: Youth and Crisis* (New York: W. W. Norton, 1968), 106.

[17] Anne-Maria Rizzuto, *The Birth of the Living God* (Chicago: University of Chicago Press, 1979), 47.

[18] Ibid., 182-88.

[19] David Heller, *The Children's God* (Chicago: University of Chicago Press, 1986). See also Martin A. Lang, *Acquiring Our Image of God* (New York: Paulist Press, 1983).

[20] Russell Baker, *Growing Up* (New York: Congdon & Weed, 1982), 61.

[21] Rizzuto, *Birth of the Living God*, 87-173.

[22] Kenneth E. Hyde, *Religion in Childhood and Adolescence* (Birmingham: Religious Education Press, 1990), 83-97.

[23] Rizzuto, *Birth of the Living God*, 87. This and the two previous paragraphs are quoted from my article "Formation of a God Representation" in *Religious Education* 91 (1996): 22-39.

[24] Helen Carboon, "God Makes Our Hearts Beat," thesis, Melbourne College of Divinity, 1999, 89-91.

Chapter 3

FAMILY AND COMMUNITY:

THE SECONDARY SOURCE FOR CHILDREN'S IMAGES OF GOD

Religion, understood as the effort of human beings to make sense out of the world and to relate themselves to whatever they consider sacred, is a normal function of the mind. That is why anthropologists have never found a group of people without a religion. In our Western, Jewish/Christian tradition, the result of this mental process of understanding the world is, at first, an untutored image of God. Then, as infants grow and respond to religious teachings and moral rules, they refine and formalize their image of God.

This secondary process of developing an understanding of God begins as soon as caregivers respond to an infant's idea of God. At the end of the previous chapter, I told how Kristin, thirty-five months old, explained to her mother how Grandpa Brice, who had died, was "in heaven with God." Her mother's reply, "Good for you, sweetheart," was an example of the secondary process, which in this instance approved her daughter's belief.

The secondary process goes on continually. Gradually children accommodate their primary image of God to whatever religious and moral instruction they receive. The period from age five to seven is of special significance. During this time children begin to observe what is happening in nature and human relations more accurately and to think about these matters more logically. For example, by age seven most children know there is no Santa Claus.[1] They retain, however, the joy of Christmas as they, like adults, enter into the fun of giving and receiving presents.

Many researchers wait until children are seven or eight years of age before inquiring about the children's images of God. At that age, students of religious development can see how the secondary process of forming an image of God has influenced children's beliefs. Also, children at this age are usually willing, even eager, to draw a picture of God, write a letter to God, or be interviewed about God.[2]

STORIES OF CHILDISH RELIGION

Throughout the previous chapter I used general statements to describe the way childish religion is formed and is then influenced by the social group in which the child is nurtured. The exact way in which religion becomes a part of one's life can only be understood by observing how it takes place in the life of a person. The stories that follow do not disclose all we would like to know about a person. Rather, the stories are from children, seven to ten years old, who have begun to formalize their image of God. It is important to note that their mental image of God is the dynamic element in their minds that extracts data from their experience and organizes it into a plausible statement about deity.

Story 1: A Concern for Fairness

Rhonda Jacobsen teaches a class on the relationship between social science and religious faith. In order to help her students gain experience in how the two are related, she requires her students to interview children about their idea of God. One child said, "God is like my principal." The adult doing the interview thought, *How sad that this child thinks of God as the final enforcer of rules.* The child, however, continued, "She [the principal] goes around the schoolyard at recess, making sure everyone gets a chance to play."[3]

At first, this idea of God seems like a childish wish to have someone in authority help the child get her turn on the swings. But on second thought we see that this girl wanted *everyone* to have a chance to play. By this statement the girl showed that her response to the use of playground equipment was based on her concern for fairness. She didn't realize that she already had a moral theory that modern philosophers call "justice as fairness."[4]

We do not have information about this girl's religious background. Her idea that God wants fairness may have been her own, or it may have come from family conversations. Whatever the source, her image of God is in harmony with some important biblical passages. God is often described as judging people on the basis of how well they used their influence and wealth to help poor or disabled people. The year of Jubilee described in Leviticus 25 was a way to help all people get a new start in life, especially the poor. Many of the psalms relate justice to fairness (Psalms 82, 96, 97, and 146 in the Contemporary English Version). Moreover, Jesus' parable of the Last Judgment is but one example of his teachings about the kind of fairness God desires (Matt 25:31-46).

Story 2: A Concern for a Human Representation of God

Robert Coles, in his comprehensive study of the spiritual aspect of children's lives, notes that Christian children have a special interest in salvation. This interest is centered in the story of Jesus' life, for children identify with his birth and his struggles. Coles uses several methods for gaining access to children's ideas of God, but being a psychiatrist he depends on interviews for his understanding of their spiritual life. The following is part of Coles's interview with ten-year-old Charles, who is trying to identify with what he thinks Jesus' life was like when he was a boy.

> "My dad is a lawyer," Charlie reminded me one day, and I wondered at that moment why he brought up the matter when we were in the midst of a talk about the Episcopal church his mother attended and the Presbyterian church his father used to attend occasionally. With some sidetracking Charlie explained himself, and here I bunch together his comments and omit most of mine: "People forget Jesus had a father as well as a mother, and he was a carpenter. I told my friend Gerry that Jesus' dad was a carpenter, and he said no, God is Jesus' father. We argued. Our minister [Episcopalian] said we're both right: Jesus had two fathers, one in heaven and one here! That's not bad! I know a lot of kids, they don't have any—I mean, their parents have split. 'It's no life,' a friend I know always says.
>
> "I think of Jesus having a dad who was a carpenter because [I had asked,] I wonder why God chose that kind of family for Him.

He must have had a reason. Right? He didn't do anything without a reason, right? That's how I see it. He must have thought to Himself: Why, I want my Son to be down there with just plain people, nothing fancy. If Jesus had grown up in a plush house and been a spoiled brat—that's the big danger in this town, my folks keep telling me!—He'd have been different. Wouldn't He? Don't you think?"

. . . . A long distraction ensued—a discussion of schoolwork and the academic life. I fended off questions as best I could, sometimes feeling uncomfortable, such as when Charlie wanted to know whether I liked "best" the students who got A's. I tried to get us over what then seemed like a barrier. But the boy had his own reasons for the inquiries he was making: "What if Jesus had trouble with something [at school], and people began laughing at him? What if a teacher really didn't like Him, really didn't give Him the time of day, really said these wisecrack remarks about Him, the way they do in school sometimes, you know? He must have felt lousy! That would have been way before He ended up feeling *real* lousy; I mean, when He was on the cross. We don't do that [crucifixion] anymore, but kids really feel left out in school, and you can see them having the worst time, and it can be the teacher's fault, or it can be our fault, kids being no good to other kids."

At a certain point it was Charlie, not I, who wanted to hurry us back to a major thesis: "Our minister told us one day [in a church sermon] that Jesus knew what it is to feel left out, and when he said that, I thought of how you can feel in school—you're alone, and no one gives a damn (that's how my father talks). When He died He knew the score here, and He must remember that—how He felt—while He's in heaven. I want to say '*up* in heaven,' but they tell us in Sunday school that we shouldn't say 'up,' because heaven isn't in the sky. Well, we asked, 'Where is it?' The teacher said its 'away from us here!' We kept asking her, 'Where? Where?' She said, 'Away, away!' Then she got mad, and we shut up! I don't care where He is; I think He remembers."

He stopped then, almost as if he himself had a little trouble remembering something. I waited. He looked at me. Still nothing. I responded, finally, to his intriguing last sentence: "What does He remember, Charlie?" He replied immediately, tersely, "Everything." I was frustrated. Clearly this boy had a lot to say about God's awareness over time—His relationship to His own life, and to ours who follow Him, we who are so distanced from His lived life.

Silence still. Charlie's head was slightly lowered. He was lost in thought, I realized, and I kept my mouth shut. Finally, after five or six long seconds, his head rose and he spoke: "He couldn't forget the way He died. He must remember the way people treated Him. You don't forget, when you're alone. I remember when we moved, and I went to school, and I didn't know anyone at first. Jesus, everyone knew Him—but they didn't like Him, they didn't believe Him, and that's even worse [than what Charlie had temporarily experienced]. So He must still remember. My mom once told me Jesus knows everything because He is God. I was supposed to pray to Him on my birthday! That's better than asking for presents, she said. So He must remember what happened to Him, if He remembers all of our birthdays! (My mom says He does!)"[5]

Story 3: A Concern for One's Self

Martin A. Lang, who has studied the way children acquire an image of God, tells of an unusual eight-year-old girl. This girl's picture of God was "an older girl in jeans, with two braids and holding balloons." Lang thought the girl had misunderstood his request. The girl insisted her drawing was of God. "God is smiling; she has balloons in her hand. I was going to draw a lollipop in her mouth. She sees everything we do." In the conversation that followed, the girl said the picture of God was her teenage sister whom she admired.[6]

Lacking any other information about this girl, we can only speculate that she has not received religious instruction. Her primary image of God seems to be a feeling of love toward people she adores. This feeling is now attached to her older sister. Like Sheila in chapter 2, her concern is for herself and her own comfort.

Story 4: A Concern for What God Has Done for Us

This picture was drawn by a seven-year-old named Valerie. Discussing the picture with Lang, Valerie said, "I drew it like that because it's the first thing I thought about. This is Jesus on the cross. That's Mary and John on one side and Mary Magdalene on the other side. The two women are crying. That's Pontius Pilate at the bottom of the hill. He's not crying because he wanted Jesus to die."

Lang's response to the interview was as follows: "Even though the scene was sorrowful, Valerie at first put a smile on Jesus' face but then erased it. That is very typical. God is usually smiling in the drawings of children. They assume he is happy—in fact, that he is basically the essence of happiness. Even though we would think Valerie's scene is depressing, for her it was a hero's story in which Jesus was doing something heroic for those around the cross."[7]

A doctoral student, Lee Bowman, after reading recent research on children's formulation of a God image, elected to study a group of children in the church she served. Her findings were like those of other researchers: that is, each child had a unique story of a God who reflected his or her concerns. One girl about eight years old said of God's home, "It's just a sky like heaven, and, like all the things you ever wanted, like a big chocolate cookie and a lot of milk and bowl full of ice cream." Then she added, "But I'd have to share it with my friends. God's so lucky. He gets to eat cookies all the time and ice cream and not get sick and not get fat." Needless to say, this child likes to eat and struggles to control her weight.

We must not, however, dismiss this chocoholic girl's idea of God as an appetite out of control. When asked about God's relation to people's troubles, she said, "I think he heals your hurts and makes them better and you feel better inside because he has the power over—probably your body. There are some things he can't control like people taking drugs and all that because, I mean, it's out of control. He's trying to fight off the bad stuff but he can't. He watches over us and makes sure we are not in trouble, and whatever happens he might get mad and he could make a thunderstorm happen or make something bad happen." She was asked, "Does a thunderstorm mean God is mad?" "No," she replied, "it doesn't mean he's mad, but the thunderstorm—like, God can't control that—or he could if he wanted—I don't know, he just wants us to be safe and everything."[8] This child is moving beyond simple ideas of God as a being who can eat what she should not eat to the consideration of the most difficult theological question: how can God be good and powerful if God lets bad things happen? She doesn't have an answer, but who does?

Not all children have stories that deify some positive attribute of human life. Bowman, like Heller and other researchers, interviewed a child who was concerned about evil. This child pictured

> God as a large, disembodied head, replete with beard and mustache and a mouth drawn in a thin line from one side of the face to the other. God sat in a swivel chair with three casters; one of his arms was outstretched, ready to pull a lever so that the Devil would fall through a trap door. The Devil was dressed up like a man because he did not want God to notice him. When asked "Why?" the child replied, "So he can turn heaven into hell." When asked if God loved her, she never answered. Other replies from this child showed considerable anxiety about her troubled relations with her caregivers.[9]

These and many other stories from children show us what they think God must be like. What we have learned from these stories may be summarized as follows.

1. Each child's primary image of God is used to interpret the child's life situation and what that child has been told about God. Moreover, the child's primary image of God as blended with religious instruction and life experience has enduring value. Gerald May, a psychiatrist who has a special interest in the spiritual aspect of life, writes as follows: "Most children and adults in our society do not relate to God. Instead, they relate to *images* of God, images that in large part have been conditioned by culture and by early childhood experiences. In most cases these images are anthropomorphized, visualizing God as a person. Also, the images are usually masculine."[10]

2. The child's primary image of God is based on emotions that develop out of relations with caregivers during infancy. The word "emotion" is now being used by developmental psychologists to mean faith (trust), hope, love, and happiness, as well as anger, fear, sadness, disgust, guilt, and shame. These emotions organize all aspects of our life into behavior: our thinking that includes how we interpret what we see and hear, our speech, and our actions.[11] Thus the formation and training of our emotions is the foundation on which we construct our image of God and the moral code by which we live.

Heller is of the opinion that a child's set of emotions, which he terms the "personality orientation," is the most influential factor in his or her description of God. Since every child's set of emotions is different, so is each child's mental image of God. It was possible, however, for Heller to place the children's God into major categories according to their dominant disposition. The categories are God, the Friendly Ghost; God, the Angry Villain; God, the Distant Thing in the Sky; God, the Lover in Heaven; The Inconsistent God; God, the Once and Future King; and God, the Therapist.[12]

3. Children become theologians as they absorb teachings about God, respond to events that happen to them, and experience an increasing ability to think and speculate. In the stories used earlier in this chapter, children identified and puzzled over the following theological issues: (1) Why are people selfish? (2) How can God be personal—connected—to all people on earth? (3) If God is love, is my experience of love the same as God? (4) Why did Jesus die on the cross? (5) If bad things happen to us, does that mean that God is mad at us? (6) If God loves us, why does the devil (evil) have so much power?

4. Children are actively engaged in a struggle to understand what behavior God approves or disapproves. The role of God in behavior is complex because conscience in its formative stage is more related to the way a child is disciplined and the relation of a child to caregivers than to the abstract notion of God. A child's linkage of God with conscience probably doesn't begin until three or four years of age and then only if the caregivers coach them to do so. Our stories show, however, that children by age seven or eight have connected approved and disapproved behavior with their idea of God. By age ten children have a moral compass by which they make decisions, but only those with a religious background relate their moral code to God.[13]

WHAT HAPPENS TO CHILDISH RELIGION?

The above summary of how children seven to ten years of age formulate what God must be like is rather encouraging. It shows that if infants experience good relations with caregivers and receive Christian education at home and church until middle childhood, they have the basic piety from which an adult understanding of God may emerge. Basic piety is of critical importance because it is the inner certainty of one's relation to God on which beliefs are formulated.[14] If one's piety is firm, then beliefs may "grow in the grace and knowledge of our Lord and Savior Jesus Christ" (2 Pet 3:18).

From middle childhood until the beginning of the teen years children tend to absorb the general ideas about God that are explained to them in the family and religious community to which they belong. After Robert Coles had spent thirty years studying children of many races under various conditions in several areas of the world, he turned his attention to their spiritual development. One of his interview questions was, "How would you describe the heart of your religion, its central message for you and for others?" Children who grew up under Christian influences talked of Jesus' role in salvation. Children who were under the influence of Islamic parents provided examples of how they wanted to surrender to the will of Allah. Jewish children by age twelve were concerned about the notion of God as a moral guide and about living according to the rules of their religion. Children of parents who were agnostic or atheistic repeated the criticisms of religion they learned from their parents.[15]

David Heller's study of children's religion produced similar results. Jewish children described God as acting in human history, especially in the life of Moses. Hindu children thought of God as a force or energy that weaves everything together. Catholic children understood God as intimately involved in family life. Baptist children tended to think of God as providing for people; yet they made a clear distinction between God and themselves.[16]

Kalevi Tamminen, after studying religious development in children and adolescents for twenty years through the use of empirical research methods, concluded that God-concepts change slowly. Moreover, the changes were more a refinement of the children's earlier conceptions of God, caused by their increasing ability to reason, than a movement to a more mature idea of God.[17]

The period from about age twelve to sixteen or seventeen is a time in which there is a great spurt of physical growth, including sexual maturation and the development of the ability to reason abstractly.[18] These developments, over which teenagers have no control, result in their movement from childhood to young adulthood.

Although adult in size, they are dependent on their parents and are legally considered to be beneath adult status. Although capable of reproducing, they are required to remain unmarried and they are urged by parents and society to be celibate. Although capable of making good rational decisions, their opinions are normally ignored. Teenagers during high school years gain approval if they do three things: keep out of trouble, make good grades, and engage in some useful leisure activity, such as a hobby or a sport.

This time between childhood and acceptance as an adult in our complex industrial culture is a time of preparation. But preparation for what? That is the question that forces teenagers to examine themselves in every aspect of their lives: interests, abilities, parental expectations, social responsibility, and moral behavior. Each of these areas of self-examination has a relation to the image of God they composed during childhood. It is no wonder, therefore, that teenagers often express doubt about their image of God or about the life and work of the church to which they belong.

Erik Erikson is one of our psychologists probably most knowledgeable of the teen years. He writes that the teenagers' situation often causes an "identity confusion" that penetrates their whole being and pulls them back to their infantile situation where time was not important, their place in the family was known, and their personal routines were well established.[19] When teenagers struggle between the unknown future of adulthood toward which they are being pushed and the childhood to which they can't return, they often go through a moratorium, a time when they seem to opt out of family and social life in order to ponder the question, "Who am I?"[20] While working through the problem of self-identity in order to become a young adult, teenagers need help from social institutions.[21]

Congregational leaders often think teenagers are the most difficult group of people to work with. Given the anxieties of the teen years, there are good reasons for that point of view. But if congregations understood that the church is exactly the place teenagers need to voice their doubts and still be accepted, then congregations would provide the kind of study and practice of Christian living that teenagers need to upgrade their image of God to adult status.

CHANGE AND CONTINUITY

The question, "What happens to childish religion?" has been answered in broad terms of human development. The studies of children's religious development that I cited do no more than illustrate that, as individuals grow, they tend to become more knowledgeable and more confident about their religion, just as they do about other matters in which they are interested. The critical issue is whether children's and teenagers' images of God will become more in harmony with God as incarnated in Jesus Christ.

There is no way to predict whether a person's childish religion will change and move toward faith in Jesus Christ as the human form of God. We know that there are many emotional factors involved, such as a desire to know God, a search for inner confidence that puts life's goals in God's perspective, a sense of guilt and shame that urge a person to become reconciled to God, or a realization that God is calling one to a specific task or vocation. Also, there are many life situations that enter into one's spiritual life, such as divorce, death of a loved one, accidents, the influence of a friend or of a peer group that helps one think through issues. Any one of these many factors alone or in some combination with other factors can be decisive in turning a person to faith in God. But almost without exception the movement to faith in God is characterized by change and continuity.

Change

By change I mean that older teenagers and adults must come to a *conscious realization* that God, as revealed in the life, death, and resurrection of Jesus Christ, is the Spirit that created us, redeems us, and guides us into a godly lifestyle. This change does not mean that a person must have a sudden religious experience, resulting in an immediate and drastically different lifestyle, although this may happen. Rather, it means that at some point in our lives we must come to a conscious realization that God is a reality in our lives and that we *want* to find and do God's will.

Our modern knowledge of human nature supports the major theme of the Bible. Old Testament writers show that human beings tend to put their interests, concerns, pleasures, and well-being ahead of God's will for human life. God called prophets, priests, leaders, and at times laypeople to witness to what God wanted God's people to do or to be. Authors of the New Testament, believing that Jesus was the Christ, had a sharper focus. Paul, the first to write about Jesus Christ, made it clear in all his letters that belief in Jesus Christ as God in human form requires a change from our psychological fears and our sociological conditioning to develop the "mind" of Jesus Christ (Phil 2:1-11; 3:12-21; Rom 8:1-11). Because Paul had a strategy for believers to develop the mind of Christ, I will discuss this matter in chapter 4, where we turn our attention to how change takes place.

Matthew's, Mark's, and Luke's accounts of the life of Jesus, written after Paul's death, all start Jesus' ministry with John the Baptist. Matthew records John's introduction of Jesus' mission and message with these words: "Repent, for the kingdom of heaven has come near" (Matt 3:2; Mark 1:4-8; Luke 3:1-14). The word "repent" *(metaneō)*, translated literally, means "you must change your mind!" Some of John's audience may have interpreted his proclamation to mean that Jesus was going to bring about and be the leader of an actual nation-like kingdom. But Jesus, considering that option to be a demonic temptation, refused (Matt 4:1-11). Rather, Jesus began his mission with the same announcement used by John: "Repent, for the kingdom of heaven has come near" (Matt 4:17). After that announcement, Jesus started to select disciples and to teach how to live according to God's will: the Sermon on the Mount (Matt 5, 6, 7).

The amount and kind of change that takes place in our lives depends on how successful we are in correcting our childish religion. Under ordinary circumstances, most of us who have been raised in Christian homes and have been active members of a congregation experience gradual change. Bits and pieces of our childish religion are discarded as we are exposed to and are stimulated by an image of God as celebrated and practiced in our congregation.

Changing our childish religion, however, with its mixture of secular and Christian values, is difficult whether it is done slowly or suddenly. This is because any change in our lifestyle that is rooted in what gives us pleasure, alleviates personal stress, or makes us *feel* that we are being religious, will be difficult to change. Moreover, there are styles of congregational life that do not encourage

Christians to change. Some congregations, for example, offer an interpretation of Christianity that supports or does not challenge values such as individualism, success as the mark of worth, competitive forms of capitalism, acquisition of wealth with little regard for obligation to society, or the superiority of one race or ethnic group over another. Other congregations may interpret Christianity to be primarily related to the family and the church. As a result, members feel little responsibility for relating the reign of God to laws, customs, or patterns of behavior that are clearly contrary to what we know to be good for the welfare of all people.

In spite of the difficulties of changing our lifestyle or the lack of concern for change exhibited by some congregations, people do come to a conscious realization of God's presence and begin to seek God's will for their lives. I will illustrate this matter with the lives of two well-known persons. It is risky to use living persons as examples, because even people with exemplary lives have some faults. I will, however, take the risk in order to show that beliefs and change are critical for what we must do to move from childish religion to faith in God.

Charles W. Colson, at age forty, had become special counsel of President Nixon and also the president's closest friend. Colson had advanced rapidly in Nixon's group of advisors because of his intense loyalty to the president and his ability to do what Nixon wanted done. *The Wall Street Journal* of October 15, 1971, labeled Colson the "Hatchet man" who did the president's dirty work. The article also contained the quip, "Colson would walk over his own grandmother if he had to" in order to reelect Nixon. Colson repeated this statement to his staff and it was in the *Washington Post* the next day.

Colson's work to reelect Nixon, including the Watergate event, had so exhausted Colson he resigned to reenter his law firm. His restlessness, however, did not vanish when he returned to private life. Somehow he thought a conversation with an old friend, Tom Phillips, president of the Raytheon Company, would help him put his life back in order. The conversation, labeled by Colson as "An Unforgettable Night," changed his life. It started when Phillips explained what Jesus Christ had come to mean to him. Phillips then urged Colson to give up his pride and turn his attention to what Christ could mean to him. Colson left Phillips's house and sat in his car for a long time. He went through an intense struggle with his lust for political power, and then experienced a "wonderful feeling of being released." He then prayed his first real prayer: "God, I don't know how to find You, but I'm going to try! I'm not much the way I am now, but somehow I want to give myself to You."[22] After his conversion, Colson spent seven months in prison for his involvement in the Watergate scandal (1974), and then formed the Prison Fellowship.

Another contemporary example is Millard Fuller. Fuller was an active church member, but he was completely absorbed in making money. He started his business career in 1960, and by 1964 he was a millionaire. To achieve so much so quickly he was seldom at home and when at home paid little attention to his family. Then, on a Saturday night in 1965, when he came home late as usual, his wife, Linda, told him his values had become different from hers. She was leaving the next day for a consultation with a minister in New York whom they both knew. In brief, Millard followed Linda to New York. They became reconciled to each other, and he resolved to change his life. Together they decided to sell all that they had, including his business, give the money away, and ask God for guidance. After several years at Koinonia Farm in Georgia and three years building houses in Zaire, the Fullers returned to the United States and visited old friends, Birdie and Bill Lytle in San Antonio. There, at Birdie's suggestion, they started what is now known as Habitat for Humanity.[23]

Many, many stories can be recited of people under ordinary or extraordinary circumstances reorienting their lives to God as revealed in Jesus Christ. An excellent collection of such stories from the Apostle Paul to Charles Colson has been collected by Hugh T. Kerr and John M. Mulder in *Conversion: The Christian Experience*. A brief introduction by the editors traces the meaning of conversion in the Bible, showing both the necessity and complexity of this experience. Although the fifty stories come from different historical periods, twenty of the stories are of people who lived in the past seventy-five years.[24] It is of critical importance that these stories along with stories of people in our congregations be shared with the whole congregation. I will discuss the reasons for such sharing in chapter 6.

Continuity

The change that comes into one's life when one is consciously aware of God's presence and becomes concerned to know and do God's will reorients one's life to please God. This does not mean that one's abilities or personal characteristics change. Colson, for example, continued to be a well-organized person with considerable ability to plan and administer large-scale projects. He applied these personal characteristics to a ministry in prisons, which he has maintained for more than twenty-five years and for which he was awarded the Templeton Prize for progress in religion. Fuller lost none of his entrepreneurial skills when he gave up his zeal for making money. He turned his energy and knowledge into helping poor people have decent housing. Today Habitat for Humanity with its slogan, "to eliminate poverty housing from the face of the earth, one home at a time," has more than 1,000 offices worldwide. Fuller himself has moved on from Habitat for Humanity to create a new ministry called the Fuller Center for Housing.

A person's move from religion to faith in God does not change that person's talents. It only changes the way talents are used.

NOTES

[1] Arnold Sameroff and Susan McDonough, "Educational Implications of Developmental Transitions, Revising the 5-to-7-Year Shift," *Phi Delta Kappan* 76/30 (November 1994): 188.

[2] For a description of how researchers explore children's images of God, see David Heller, *The Children's God* (Chicago: University of Chicago Press, 1986), 5-18; 152-56. See also Robert Coles, *The Spiritual Life of Children* (Boston: Houghton Mifflin Company, 1990), 22-40.

[3] Douglas Jacobsen, "Inclusive and Discerning?" *Christian Century* 116/3 (21-28 April 1999): 441.

[4] "Justice as fairness" is a major moral philosophy supported by John Rawls. See Brian Barry and Matt Matravers, "Justice," *Encyclopedia of Philosophy*, vol. 5 (London: Routledge, 1998), 144-45.

[5] Coles, *Spiritual Life of Children*, 209-12. If the reader is interested in the relation of psychoanalysis and religion, chapter 1 is an excellent overview of that subject. The study of children's ideas of God is rather new in the psychology of human development. Coles's method, which he presents in chapter 2, is of critical importance for appreciating the results of his work.

[6] Martin A. Lang, *Acquiring Our Image of God* (New York: Paulist Press, 1983), 78.

[7] Ibid., 77.

[8] Lee Willey Bowman, "Discerning the Spirit: An Exploration into the Evaluation of Religious Experience," Doctor of Ministry project report, Austin Presbyterian Theological Seminary, 1997, 9-11.

[9] Ibid., 10-16. See also Heller, *Children's God*, 80-83.

[10] Gerald G. May, *Will and Spirit* (New York: Harper and Row, 1982), 139.

[11] Ross A. Thompson, "Socioemotional Development," *Encyclopedia of Human Behavior*, vol. 14 (San Diego CA: Academy Press, 1944), 275-80. See also Avshalom Caspi, "Personality Development Across the Life Course," *Handbook of Child Psychology*, vol. 3 (New York: John Wiley and Sons, 1998), 311-71. Daniel Goleman considers emotions and thinking as two separate but interrelated matters within the brain. In normal everyday situations, the emotions function so easily we seldom note their presence or power in what we say or do. If, however, an emergency occurs when we must act quickly, the emotions "hijack" reason. Then we realize that "our emotions have a mind of their own, one which can hold views quite independent of our rational mind" (*Emotional Intelligence* [New York: Bantam Books, 1995], 20).

[12] Heller, *Children's God*, 76-94.

[13] Robert Coles, Project Director, *Girl Scouts Survey on the Beliefs and Moral Values of America's Children* (New York: Girl Scouts of the United States of America, 1989), xiv-xv.

[14] James M. Gustafson, *Ethics from a Theocentric Perspective*, vol. 1 (Chicago: University of Chicago Press, 1981), 257. An excellent definition of faith—what I have called "Basic piety"—and its relation to belief is in the report written by Craig Dykstra, *Growing in the Life of Christian Faith* (Louisville: Theology and Worship Ministry Unit, Presbyterian Church [U.S.A.], 1989), 5-19.

[15] Coles, *Spiritual Life of Children*, 202-303.

[16] Heller, *Children's God*, 18-39.

[17] Kalevi Tamminen, "Changing God-Concepts in Childhood and Adolescence: Empirical Results, Methodological Problems," *Panorama* 8 (1996): 115-36.

[18] David Moshman, "Cognitive Development Beyond Childhood," *Handbook of Child Psychology*, vol. 2 (New York: John Wiley and Sons, 1998), 972-73.

[19] Erik H. Erikson, *Identity: Youth and Crisis* (New York: W. W. Norton, 1968), 179-88.

[20] Ibid., 191-93.

[21] Ibid., 189.

[22] Charles W. Colson, *Born Again* (Old Tappan NJ: Chosen Books, 1976).

[23] Millard Fuller and Diane Scott, *Love in the Mortar Joints* (Piscataway NJ: New Win Publishing, 1980), 39-53.

[24] Hugh T. Kerr and John M. Mulder, *Conversions* (Grand Rapids: Eerdmans Publishing Company, 1983).

Part Two

A CONGREGATIONAL STRATEGY FOR CHRISTIAN FORMATION

Chapter 4

THE PERSUASIVE POWER OF CONGREGATIONS

By following the pattern of influence, we have two major reasons to reexamine the way congregations nurture the rising generation. The first is the lack of support from our culture. The second is information from the social sciences that children acquire mental images of God and character traits in the first few years of life while they are under the direct influence of their parents.

GOAL OF DISCIPLESHIP

We should set the goal of discipleship as Jesus did when a lawyer asked him to do so. Jesus said, "You shall love the Lord your God with all your heart, and with all your soul, and with all your mind." And "You shall love your neighbor as yourself" (Matt 22:37-40). In the Bible the meanings of the words "heart," "soul," and "mind" overlap. Today the word "mind" means thinking, reasoning, and knowledge, so I'll use this meaning to distinguish this part of one's self from the affections.

The way to work toward this goal is for the congregation to nurture its members, adults as well as children. To nurture is to have a concern for the whole person: affections as well as the mind. The affections or sentiments (emotionally charged attitudes) are character traits such as honesty, sympathy, concern for the welfare of others, forgiveness, trustworthiness, and kindness. Nurturing the affections is of critical importance because they are lodged deep within a person's being and because there is considerable evidence that emotions have power to influence or control a person's speech and conduct.

CONGREGATIONS

I think our situation is similar in some respects to that faced by the Apostle Paul, the first writer in the New Testament to formulate a strategy for communicating faith in God in a hostile social environment. He knew from his ancient Jewish wisdom that a community (synagogue) was necessary to form and maintain beliefs and a lifestyle different from the surrounding culture. Such a faith community would not reflect its beliefs perfectly, but it would provide mental, emotional, and material support for its members. In Paul's writings, such communities shared aspects of the surrounding culture, but church members were expected to develop a fellowship based on beliefs about Jesus Christ.

Our situation is dissimilar to Paul's first-century churches in that our culture was founded on Christian principles, and Christianity in various forms continues to be the religion of about 75 percent of Americans. Moreover, deep within the mentality of Americans are religiously rooted moral principles to which the Rev. Martin Luther King, Jr., for example, could successfully appeal to secure civil rights for African Americans. Paul Tillich, a refugee theologian from Nazi Germany, observed a latent Christian mentality in the United States formed by culture but not secured by theological beliefs. We should be thankful for this latent Christianity but should not expect people with this mentality to become Christian disciples unless they become active members of a congregation.

Underlying the historical and sociological survey in previous chapters is a clue for reinvigorating the nurturing work of a congregation. The clue is the critical importance of beliefs—what people truly believe govern their lifestyle. People with deeply held Christian beliefs will produce congregations that seek God's guidance, parents who train their children from birth in a Christian lifestyle, and adults who are concerned for the welfare of all people in the community. The converse is also true. People with uncertain or confusing Christian beliefs will produce congregations and parents who are unable to relate the meaning of their faith to others.

Beliefs are generated by individuals, but beliefs endure only when they are shared by a group of people who value them enough to pass them on to their children. Beliefs held in common by members of a congregation have unusual persuasive power because they are about the nature of and relation to God; they explain how God wants people to live; and they define the nature of life after death. This chapter, therefore, is first about the psychological power of deeply held beliefs.

After illustrating the misuse of congregational power, I will use the letters of the Apostle Paul to show how deeply held Christian beliefs must relate to the problems and situations in a congregation as well as to generic human conditions such as self-centeredness, which becomes a part of every person's experience in early childhood.[1] Thus, the first step in revitalization of congregational nurture is the formation of a group of people who are guided by Christian beliefs.

PSYCHOLOGY: POWER OF BELIEFS

Kurt Lewin, a social psychologist, is reported to have said, "Learning is a new belonging." By this he indicated that learning and belonging to a group take place simultaneously. If you want to learn something, you should join a group of people who are doing or studying what you want to learn. The quickest and best way to learn a language is to join a group of people who speak and write that language. Likewise, if you want to learn how to rob banks, join a gang of successful bank robbers. By participating with people who speak a language or rob banks, you acquire the knowledge, skills, attitudes, and confidence necessary to do the same. The key word is "belonging."

Belonging to a group also empowers members to live according to the beliefs and values of the group. When you invest yourself in the life and work of a group, you begin to think and act according to what the group believes and does. Thus, belonging to a group can create an enormous personal dedication to the group. This identification with a group is often displayed in a person's jewelry, clothing, or special forms of greeting. Even when members of a group are off to themselves, their group's beliefs and values guide their thoughts and actions.

There are, of course, many kinds of groups to which people belong. Each group has influence according to the amount of allegiance a member invests in the group. Congregations, because of their beliefs about God, tend to develop intense loyalty among members who participate on a regular basis.

I must note that the power that comes from congregating is a psychological fact, not a religious matter. The psychological power that is generated in groups appears in political, social, civic, and neighborhood clubs or societies as well as in Christian congregations.

The power of a congregation to control the lives of its members under a dynamic leader can produce tragic results. The Reverend James W. Jones, for example, formed The People's Temple in California and proclaimed himself the Messiah. He moved the entire congregation to Guyana. While investigating the group on November 18, 1978, a congressman who thought members of the group were being held in the congregation against their will was killed. When that happened, Jones ordered his followers to commit suicide and 909 did so. More recently David Koresh, who claimed to be Jesus Christ, led his group of believers to a compound east of Waco, Texas, to await the end of the world. There on April 19, 1993, he persuaded 86 members to die with him rather than to surrender to the Federal Bureau of Alcohol, Tobacco, and Firearms. On March 26, 1997, in a mansion near San Diego, police found 39 bodies of the Heaven's Gate religious cult. Led by Marshall Applewhite, the group gave up their lives, believing that their souls would be picked up by a spaceship following the Hale-Bopp comet.

The above stories are examples of how a leader with a psychopathic mind can form a congregation. With the power generated in a group holding common beliefs, members become willing to give up their lives for their beliefs. In less dramatic ways some congregations today use their group psychological power to control members' recreation, dress, political opinions, and sometimes their vocational choices. How to guard against false prophets or misguided beliefs and practices has always been a problem. The Old Testament contains many references to false prophets. Matthew, Mark, and Luke all quote Jesus as saying false prophets would always appear.

Most congregations can identify the demonic power of false prophets and the misguided beliefs of religious groups that have only a superficial knowledge of the Bible. The problem most congregations have is how to be a Christian community in an institutional form. I think the problem is unsolvable because it is rooted in human nature. Perhaps it would be more accurate to classify this situation as a dilemma. The only way to preserve beliefs is to have a well-defined tradition and a means of communicating that tradition to succeeding generations. The resulting organization, be it a loosely regulated informal association or a well-defined social institution, will become domesticated. This happens because there must be standards for membership, rules for selection of leaders, places to meet, money to be raised and policies for uses of money, means for the preparation and approval of educational materials and doctrinal statements, procedures for dealing with conflicts, and many other matters essential for the church to endure. Each one of the matters essential for Christians to prosper as a congregation is an opening for human pride to express itself. Church leaders may become more concerned about their status in the church than about their roles as teachers and pastors. Standards for membership may be so lax that the church becomes little more than a social club or so strict the church assumes it knows who is right before God. More money may be spent to glorify the church building than on the mission of the church. Belief statements may be more attuned to what will attract church members than they are to what has been revealed about God in Jesus Christ. Sacraments may be interpreted and used more in terms of what they will do to tie people to the church than in terms of how they relate people to God.[2] The corroding influence of pride—the root of sin—is the reason institutionalized religion seldom improves with age.

CONGREGATIONS: WHERE BELIEFS ARE LEARNED

Every letter we have from the Apostle Paul was addressed to a congregation. Even his brief personal letter to Philemon about Philemon's runaway slave was addressed to "the church in your house" (Phlm 2). Although Paul preached and taught that it is individuals who must accept Christ as their Savior and live a Christ-centered life, he formed believers into congregations. He did so because gathering believers into a community that meets regularly for worship and instruction was what he knew from his experience in a synagogue. The synagogue was well established as the place for Jews to gather as they lived in a social environment hostile to, or different from, their beliefs and lifestyle.[3] According to Wayne Meeks,

> There are in fact a number of similarities between the Jewish communities in the Greco-Roman cities and the Pauline groups that grew up alongside them. . . . The sorts of activities in the meetings were also probably similar, including scripture reading and interpretation, prayers, common meals, but in neither case the sacrifices that were characteristic in pagan cults. . . . Most important, the Pauline Christians took over the scripture, large and basic parts of the belief system, and a great many norms and traditions, either whole or with some modification, from Greek-speaking synagogues.[4]

Paul, however, did not think that when Christians gathered for worship and instruction the meeting was a place to gossip, to argue, to get ahead in the line for food, or to drink too much wine (1 Cor 11:17-22). Rather, Paul rooted worship in the Lord's Supper and wrote that partaking of the bread and wine was a *Koinōnia* in the body and blood of Christ (1 Cor 10:14-17). Paul's use of the word *Koinōnia* introduced something new in the act of Christian worship.[5] The King James Version of the Bible (1611) translated *Koinōnia* as "communion," a term that has endured. The New Revised Standard Version translated it "sharing," emphasizing the connection between believers and Christ. *Koinōnia* is difficult to translate, but the idea is that believers have a relationship with Christ through identification with his body given in death and resurrected by God. People who believed Jesus was the Christ were blessed with a tie that bonded them together in a "fellowship of kindred minds."

This idea of believers meeting to experience a personal relation with Christ by symbols (bread and wine) of a bodily connection is profoundly spiritual and practical. If our body does not function properly, we promptly attend to its needs. Paul thought of our physical body as the home of the Spirit of God; so believers should honor their bodies as they would honor a guest in their home.

Contrariwise, persons who misuse their bodies are sinning against the Spirit of God (1 Cor 6:15-20).

This idea of believers' bodies being connected to the body of Christ as celebrated in the Lord's Supper was extended by Paul to mean that in Christ's absence, believers were the body of Christ (1 Cor 12:27). Thus, the church's mission was to continue the ministry and work of Christ until he returned. This led Paul to explain how the church, made up of people with different interests and abilities, could continue Christ's ministry. The basic idea is simple. A person's body has many parts, each with a well-defined function. One part does not feel superior to another, for it takes all parts to make the body function effectively. So members of the church differ, but each adds something to the whole community that looks to Christ, the head, for guidance.

This theological description of the church as the body of Christ was written to help the Corinthian church overcome the strong differences in beliefs that were dividing the congregation into warring groups. Although this description of that church was accurate, it was not a reflection of God's desire. Paul concluded his description with the words, "And I will show you a still more excellent way" (to be the church) (1 Cor 12:31). He continued with the well-known poem on love that defines God's relationship to us and should characterize our relationships to each other.

After showing that love was the "more excellent way" for church members to relate to each other in working through issues that divided them, Paul launched into a discussion of the issue about which there was bitter disagreement—speaking in tongues. Throughout Paul's treatment of this issue, he considered the congregation the most important factor in its resolution. He wrote that whatever was done in the congregation must be done to edify, to build up, to encourage, to console, or to instruct the members. Paul did everything he could do in a letter, including a suggested compromise to hold the congregation together because it was the body of Christ (1 Cor 14).

Where did Paul get such a profound appreciation of the congregation as being the body of Christ? We do not know for sure, but we can infer that this belief came out of his own experience. Paul wrote that after his conversion he did not go to Jerusalem to confer with the disciples. Rather, he went to Arabia for three years (Gal 1:15-19). There are reasons to believe that Paul went to Arabia because the Damascene Christians had established a church there made up of Gentiles.[6] I assume that Paul experienced the Spirit of Christ there, which helped him put aside the religion he learned as a child and practiced as an adult (Acts 8:1-3; 9:1-2). Because Paul's conversion was so dramatic, we often fail to appreciate the struggle he had with his pharisaical beliefs. Any one of the following particular beliefs would be difficult to change; yet Paul "put an end to" each one. As a Pharisee Paul knew and probably prayed as follows (Acts 26:4-6):

> There are three blessings one must pray daily:
> Blessed (art thou), who did not make me a gentile
> Blessed (art thou), who did not make me a woman
> Blessed (art thou), who did not make me an uncultured person.[7]

Paul "put an end to" his prejudice against Gentiles, women, and uncultured people because he learned that in Christ there is no longer Jew or Greek, male or female, slave or free. All who believe in Christ and belong to him are of equal value (Gal 3:23-29). In addition, Paul no longer believed that a person became right with God by obeying religious laws. Rather, one became righteous by accepting the love of God as shown in Jesus Christ (Rom 7:7–8:17). He also rejected the practice of killing Jews who disagreed with him (Gal 1:13-14). He learned to respect people with other religions, especially Jews, in order to present to them the good news about Jesus Christ (1 Cor 9:19-23; Acts 17:16-31). I could cite other changes in Paul's life such as his reconsideration of educational achievement. Whereas as a Pharisee he was proud of his philosophical knowledge, as a Christian he placed a higher value on his relation to Jesus Christ (1 Cor 1:18-31).

This process of working through one's immature ideas of God is something all adults need to do. Although it may be done without much help from others, we, like Paul, can do it most effectively in a congregation. The process takes time—Paul took three years—as we become conscious of what we need to change, and it takes continuous support from a group of Christians who are likewise struggling to be a new creation (2 Cor 5:16-21).

Paul's mystical feeling that the congregation was the body of Christ did not mean individuals were relieved of responsibility for their lives. Paul always addressed individuals as part of a congregation. His phrase was, "Now you are the body of Christ and individually members of it" (1 Cor 12:27; see also Rom 12:4-5). It was by participation in congregations that believers were to acquire the mind of Christ (Phil 2:2-5; 3:15; Col 3:1-2), to "grow up . . . into Christ" (Eph 4:14-16), and to relate to Christ in such a way they could "teach and admonish one another in all wisdom . . ." (Col 3:12-17).

BELIEFS AS A QUEST FOR RIGHTEOUSNESS

Theology, being a human enterprise, is always rooted in culture. So let's take a few minutes to get our bearings. We in the Western world live in what has been labeled "postmodern" times. This term is used not so much to define our era as it is an indication that the assumptions underlying Western culture do not hold much promise for the future. The Enlightenment, which began in the eighteenth century, ushered in the modern era. The major assumptions of the Enlightenment were that humankind was developing and improving over time; that individuals had rights, especially for happiness; and that reason, applied to human life and nature, would slowly but surely provide control over human life and our environment.

The Enlightenment has produced many good things for Western civilization. Democratic forms of government that provide justice and care for citizens are far superior to autocratic rulers. Other developments such as universal education, instant communication, machines that do hard work, and advances in medical practice can be cited as resulting directly or indirectly from Enlightenment assumptions.[8] We should be thankful for developments that make life easier and more interesting or that provide opportunity for people to be secure and feel worthwhile. The problem with the Enlightenment was its optimistic view of human nature: the assumption that the use of reason would produce reasonable people or that the fruits of science would always be used to better humankind. We now know that human nature has not changed. Advances in science have been used to build more efficient ways of waging wars. More people were killed in twentieth-century wars than in any other century in recorded history. Moreover, the most deadly wars were fought between nations with the most advanced science and the highest level of educated citizens. Poverty and its allies—crime, ignorance, and hopelessness—remain a serious problem in our wealthiest nations. Prejudice between races or ethnic groups exists in almost every nation on earth.

The culture of the United States at the beginning of the twenty-first century is different from the Greek/Roman culture of the first century in which Paul lived. The issue is not a comparison of our understanding of the earth and its place in space, our knowledge of nature and biology, our democratic form of government, our science, or our communication systems with Paul's lack of knowledge of these matters. Rather, the issue is the extent to which our human situation is different from that of the first century. In this regard I see no difference. Our self-centeredness, our pride, our anxiety about death, our propensity to value success, wealth, pleasure, or personal acclaim is different only in the way we express these human traits. In fact, we can go back about a thousand years before Paul's time and find that the human traits Moses identified as destructive of human life are still our problem. These traits are the anger or selfishness that ruin family life, violent actions against others including murder, inability to control sexual urges, taking what we want regardless of who owns it, lying to protect ourselves or to gain what we want, and envy that destroys the mutual respect and assistance that is the basis of human community (Exod 20:12-17).

In general terms the problem of how to interpret and to live the Christian life in our secular society is the same as Paul faced in the pagan culture of the Roman Empire. Paul's solution to this problem was to focus attention on the congregation. The congregation and its members influenced each other, but one was not more important than the other. Both congregations and members were to be oriented by Christ. This orientation means that both the congregation and the individual are in a struggle to put away immature ideas of God and "press on toward the goal for the prize of the heavenly call of God in Christ Jesus" (Phil 3:14). We must remind ourselves that this quotation (and the paragraph in which it is located) was written to a congregation and its members.

Given the above understanding of the symbiotic relation between congregations and members, what holds them together and causes them to grow up in their faith? Or what are the areas in which congregations must struggle in order to grow up in their faith? The answer is made up of the following essential beliefs: (1) to know God as revealed in Jesus Christ, (2) to take responsibility for bringing about God's will for the world, and (3) to engage in a lifelong struggle to live a Christian life.

Belief 1: To Know God as Revealed in Jesus Christ

Paul learned to know Jesus Christ through an intense personal experience. Paul never used the term "conversion." He described his experience with Christ as a "revelation" (Gal 1:11-12) and himself as one to whom Christ "appeared" after the resurrection (1 Cor 15:8). Paul cited his personal experience with Christ to prove his authority as an apostle rather than to set an expectation that others have the same kind of experience. Paul did not change from being irreligious to being religious; he did not change from being immoral to being moral; nor did he change from one religion to another. Paul had always been a religious, moral person. What changed was his image of God, and this changed his mind about almost everything.

Although conversion in some stylized form does not seem to be Paul's aim, he was certain that to be saved a person must have faith in Jesus Christ. When writing to Jews, Paul showed respect for the Mosaic Law, saying it "was our disciplinarian until Christ came, so that we might be justified by faith. But now that faith has come, we are no longer subject to a disciplinarian, for in Christ Jesus you are all children of God through faith" (Gal 3:24-26). When writing to Gentiles Paul started with sin as a human condition and then explained, "For by grace you have been saved through faith, and this is not your own doing; it is the gift of God—not the result of works, so that no one may boast" (Eph 2:8-9).

One can learn about Christianity in schools, from reading about it, from conversation with believers, or from attending church worship. But knowing about Christianity is not the same as knowing God as revealed by Jesus. Faith in Christian terms is not something we have as we "have" an education or "have" good health. Rather it is a relational term. We "have" faith in Christ or we "have" faith that in Christ we are properly related to God. Paul wrote that, as a result of his preaching and teaching, he wanted to "present every one mature in Christ" (Col 1:28). So grown-up or mature faith was not a stage of life or an attainment but was a relationship with Christ. Then, through the relationship, a person would grow up into a Christian lifestyle.

Belief 2: To Take Responsibility for Bringing about God's Will for the World

Jesus, according to Matthew, Mark, and Luke, spent much of his time explaining the kingdom of God. That kingdom, embedded in the Lord's Prayer, means the "rule" of God as explained in the next phrase: "Your will be done, on earth as it is in heaven" (Matt 6:10).

Paul's way of relating to the rulership of God was to consider himself a servant of Christ, which was how he introduced himself or referred to himself in almost all of his letters (Rom 1:1). When he defended himself to the church at Corinth against his opponents, he asked, "Are they ministers of Christ?" (2 Cor 11:23). If his opponents could not pass this test, they were not trying to bring about God's rule in the world. Paul also used the master/servant motif in his letter to the church at Philippi. After identifying himself as a servant of Christ, he used Christ's life as an example of obedience to God. He then urged his readers to have the same mind toward Christ as Christ had toward God (Phil 2:1-12). Paul considered the church as a continuation of Christ's ministry in and to the world.

Belief 3: To Engage in a Lifelong Struggle to Live a Christian Life

Paul's longest and most systematic theological essay is his letter to the Romans. The purpose was to introduce himself and to express a desire to stop in Rome on his way to Spain (Rom 15:22-29). After a careful discussion of our human condition and Christ's role in salvation, Paul stops with an "amen." He then turns to how believers are to live. The transition from theology to a Christian lifestyle is often quoted: "I appeal to you therefore, brothers and sisters, by the mercies of God, to present your bodies as a living sacrifice, holy and acceptable to God, which is your spiritual worship" (Rom 12:1).

As a practical matter today, that verse means we must identify the secular values learned in childhood and struggle to replace them with a lifestyle in harmony with God's will. One way to do this is to obtain the help of a minister, a psychologist, or person who has been trained as a spiritual director. These specialists help many people who want guidance and support as they struggle to live with a grown-up image of God.

Paul believed that knowing the truth about God should always result in a life reflecting God's concerns. His method was to describe how Christian people should relate to each other and to non-Christians. He assumed that such a description would encourage Christians to struggle more intently to imitate Christ as he did (1 Cor 11:1). Thus, Paul included in each of his letters instructions on how Christians should live. Some of these instructions take up large portions of a letter. In addition to Romans 12–16, Paul's longer sections on the Christian lifestyle are Ephesians 4–6; Philippians 2–3; Galatians 5:13–6:10; and Colossians 3–4:6.

I hope you have noticed that these three beliefs are stated in terms of goals toward which Christians strive. Theological beliefs are an effort to understand and relate to God. This means that traditional theological statements that have been tested and refined through the centuries form our Christian life. New conditions and discoveries, however, require openness to God's will regarding newly created issues. This open stance toward some traditional beliefs creates uncertainty. As a result there is always a period of time when congregations struggle to formulate a satisfactory statement about situations not referred to in the Bible or by tradition. Slavery, the ordination of women, capitalism, or democracy are examples of changes to which most Christian churches have formulated a response.

Some of the above issues have not yet been resolved to the satisfaction of all Christians, and newer issues from the advances in medical science are just emerging. What is important for our purpose is that congregations are the place where issues are discussed and where Christian beliefs are tentatively formed. American denominations often formulate a theological response to a new situation through their national governing body. This does not mean that all congregations of a denomination accept the official theological statement. Rather, members of a congregation discuss the new situation and the proposed denominational response, and they either accept it, reject it, ignore it, or develop their own theological statement. If a congregation considers its beliefs to be out of harmony with the official position of its denomination, it will seek a way to become independent or attach itself to a denomination sympathetic to its beliefs. If individual members of a congregation become disenchanted with its beliefs, they leave and seek a church more in harmony with their own beliefs.

In brief, beliefs and the lifestyle they produce are the clue for understanding what a congregation will communicate to its members and their children. Since congregations have considerable power to persuade, it is of critical importance for Christian congregations to seek first the kingdom (rulership) of God as revealed by Christ in order to have the beliefs that result in an appropriate lifestyle.[9]

Modern congregations, like the ones described in the New Testament, are made up of members who have some generic human traits such as pride, avarice, intemperance, or envy as well as attitudes and values they acquired from their culture. Thus, we must consider congregations as well as individual members to be in a struggle to interpret God's will for new situations and a struggle to make daily decisions in accord with what we know to be God's expectation.

NOTES

[1] See chapter 3.

[2] Max Weber wrote that religion starts with a charismatic leader but the followers "routinize" it in an institutional form. See H. H. Gerth and C. Wright Mills, eds., *From Max Weber: Essays in Sociology* (New York: Oxford University Press, 1958), 250. Thomas F. O'Dea in his *The Sociology of Religion* (Englewood Cliffs NJ: Prentice-Hall, 1966) described five dilemmas institutionalized religion must endure. I illustrated how O'Dea's analysis was true of the New Testament church in my *How Faith Matures* (Louisville: Westminster/John Knox Press, 1989), 66-72.

[3] For an excellent account of why the Jewish and Christian religions are centered in congregations, see Bruce C. Birch, "Memory in Congregational Life," in *Congregations: Their Power to Form and Transform*, ed. C. Ellis Nelson (Atlanta: John Knox Press, 1988), 20-42.

[4] Wayne A. Meeks, *The First Urban Christians* (New Haven: Yale University Press, 1983), 80-81.

[5] "Lord's Supper," *The Anchor Bible Dictionary*, 1992 ed., 4:364.

[6] "Paul," *The Anchor Bible Dictionary,* 1992 ed., 5:188

[7] Quoted by John E. Alsup, "Imagining the New," *Austin Seminary Bulletin* (Spring 1990): 95.

[8] For a fuller description of the way the Enlightenment affected "American culture," see my *How Faith Matures,* 21-41.

[9] See Anthony B. Robinson, *What's Theology Got to Do with It?* (Herndon VA: Alban Institute Press, 2006) for a more detailed analysis of how a congregation's beliefs may influence its members to practice a Christian lifestyle.

Chapter 5

INFORMAL PROCESSES OF NURTURING

The previous chapter left us with the conclusion that a congregation's ability to nurture faith in God is directly related to the clarity of its beliefs and the degree to which its members form a lifestyle based on those beliefs. That chapter concluded with a listing of some of our generic human traits that corrupt our being and prevent us from doing what God desires. Congregations, therefore, must always struggle to be oriented to God's purpose.

The Apostle Paul described this struggle to the church at Corinth in these words: "But we have this treasure [the gospel] in clay jars [human beings], so that it may be made clear that this extraordinary power belongs to God and does not come from us" (2 Cor 4:7). Paul was so confident about the treasure we have in Christ that he did not allow the frail nature of congregations to discourage him (2 Cor 4:8-18). Although the social contexts and sizes of congregations founded by Paul are different from our era, the task is the same: to proclaim and teach about Christ "so that we may present everyone mature in Christ" (Col 1:28; 4:12). This idea of maturity is also referred to in 1 Corinthians 2:6; 14:20; Ephesians 4:13; Philippians 3:15; and Hebrews 5:14.

Given Paul's example of centering the formation of Christian maturity in congregations and our modern understanding of the power of belonging to a community, (1) how can we help church leaders become more aware of the natural processes of nurturing that occur in congregations, and (2) how can we use those processes more effectively? The answers to these questions involve how the

ethos of a congregation relates to self-understanding and how efforts
to change ethos are also a nurturing process.

ETHOS AS FORMATION

The ethos of a congregation refers to the general characteristics that
give it a distinct nature. This does not indicate that each congregation is unique, for, as we shall see in the following cases, researchers
often classify churches according to types. It does mean, however,
that if a congregation is classified as a "family" type, its way of being
a family is special. This is because factors such as the personality of
leaders, location, history, size, program, and style of worship give its
"family" character a particular flavor.

What is of critical importance for our purpose is the way the
ethos of a congregation nurtures its members. The word "nurture"
includes everything that defines, encourages, or sustains the spiritual
life of church members. Belonging to a congregation and being a
part of its community is a gentle but powerful way of being influenced by its members. The clearest example of how the ethos of a
congregation forms the beliefs and values of its members is found in
cults such as I mentioned at the beginning of the previous chapter. I
doubt that James Jones, David Koresh, or Marshall Applewhite
needed any formal program of education to train new members or
children in their beliefs and lifestyle. What the cult stood for was
proclaimed and modeled by everyone in the community. To belong
to the cult was to embody what made it a community.

The ethos of mainstream Protestant congregations is also powerful, but its ethos is more complex than that of a cult. This is so
because members of mainstream congregations tend to hold on to
the values, habits, and beliefs from their childhoods, from their
social relations, and from their workplaces. The exact configuration
of what church members bring with them is unique, but there is
enough similarity among members' beliefs to create an ethos that is
communicated both to children and new members.

VARIOUS FORMS OF CONGREGATIONAL ETHOS

These chapters have assumed that we are living in a culture that is
becoming increasingly secular. I reviewed some of the data for this
opinion in chapter 1. Robert Wuthnow, professor of sociology and

director of the Center for the Study of Religion at Princeton University, shares this judgment of American society. In general terms, Wuthnow believes that about 25 percent of the United States population is devout; about 25 percent is secular; and about 50 percent is mildly interested in religion. He describes our nation's religious mind as follows:

> We are in some ways a very religious country, especially compared to Western Europe. But we're of two minds, and the other mind is that we really are pretty secular. We are very much a country of consumers and shoppers, and we're quite materialistic. And as long as we can kind of paste together a sense of control through our ordinary work and our ordinary purchases, we're pretty happy to do that.[1]

Mainstream Protestant congregations range all the way from mainly devout members to mildly interested people. Some congregations can easily become enamored with secular values, such as success measured in terms of size or power as judged by wealth or public acclaim. A congregation is not a solution to the secular nature of American society unless it is in an active struggle to be "the body of Christ."

When members of a congregation share their beliefs about God, they produce an ethos or disposition that can be described in a general way. Carl Dudley has suggested various ways of categorizing congregations. One way is to use biblical images such as the church as "the bride of Christ" (2 Cor 11:2) or, as Paul often did, the church as "the body of Christ."[2] Others who study congregations prefer to group them according to their location, ethos, or purpose. Dudley uses a typology based on how members of a congregation understand it. This method results in thinking of congregations according to their major interest expressed in words such as family, nurture, denomination, sanctuary, citizen, servant, social prophet, or evangelist. Dudley's fuller description of each of these types of churches shows that although a congregation has a distinctive character, it also has a traditional set of activities and study groups.[3]

During the past twenty-five years there has been a vast expansion of congregational studies. For example, a team of researchers at Hartford, Connecticut, surveyed 413 Protestant, Catholic, and Jewish congregations in that area. After reporting in general terms about those congregations, they made a comprehensive study of ten. If you were to read their description of any one of the ten congregations, you would gain a rather clear idea of what its major interest was.[4]

Don Browning provides us with a fine example of how much one learns from the ethos of a congregation. Browning, on his first Sunday visit to the Apostolic Church of God located near the University of Chicago, noted the parking lot's ushers, the neighborhood, the church buildings, music (orchestra, choir, and congregational singing), sermon, social concerns, and many other facts about this church's program. In his first interview with Helen Barnes, a psychologist, he experienced the guiding theme of the congregation. Barnes told him she believed God was doing something special in bringing him to her church. She said her custom was to invoke an experience of the Holy Spirit for everyone with whom she came in contact. She proceeded to pray with Browning, for she was confident that he—a University of Chicago professor—could become a "sanctified saint."[5]

Nelle Slater has written an excellent account of the Church of the Covenant, a conservative church of a thousand members located in the Midwest. This church, after a year of study and planning, became a sanctuary for political refugees from El Salvador at a time when that was contrary to U.S. immigration policy. As a result, the church was featured in national newspapers and on an NBC television newscast. To be a member of that congregation during the year of study was a profound educational experience because everyone knew that at the end of the year they would be expected to vote for or against becoming a sanctuary church.[6]

Stephen Warner, a sociologist, spent a year participating in every aspect of the Mendocino California Presbyterian Church, a church he had known from his annual family visits to Mendocino. His report of this congregation's move from a liberal to an evangelical orientation is a classic study of how the ethos of a church can change and what that process means to its members.[7]

Gary Dorsey, a journalist, spent several years as a participant-observer of First Church in Windsor, Connecticut. He attended almost every meeting of every group in the church, talked frequently with officers, and interviewed most of the members in their homes.

He concluded that this church was a diverse collection of people: some took their faith in God seriously; some had only an intellectual interest; some considered the church and its work important; and some were seekers for truth about God but put the church's needs in second place. Such an assembly of people functioned like a club where the members shared social values but reserved their beliefs about God to themselves.[8]

Penny E. Becker studied twenty-three Catholic, Jewish, and Protestant congregations in the Oak Park, Illinois, area. She was interested in how these congregations handled conflict. Her report is a wonderful example of an outsider gaining an understanding of how a congregation understands itself and how members communicate their beliefs to each other in a deliberate but informal manner.[9]

Nile Harper has a special interest in urban churches that are concerned to go beyond charity by working for justice in their community. Harper located 28 Catholic and Protestant churches ranging in size from 125 to 15,000 members in 15 major cities throughout the United States. What is of paramount importance in reading the stories of these churches is the way each congregation found a social need in their community—such as affordable housing, health care, employment opportunities, quality of public schools, working conditions in sweatshops, or economic development—and started a sustained effort to bring about desirable changes. The stories describe how each congregation taught through its worship, classes, official board actions, and allocation of funds that to be a member one would be expected to help bring about social justice.[10]

Dynamics of Congregational Ethos

If you should read the full description of the life and mission of the congregations noted above or add the story of a congregation you know well, you would probably agree that church life is dynamic. The dynamism is created by the interaction of members with each other. The results of members' interaction depend on the congregation's situation. An influx of new members may create interest in new projects. A new pastor's vision of what the congregation should be could result in a different allocation of funds. Or a church could unexpectedly receive a large sum of money from the will of a deceased member and find that many proposals emerge for its use.

Regardless of any particular situation, the interaction of church members takes place whenever they meet. Most conversations occur before and after worship or classes, in committee meetings, during social events, and in a more formal way during the official governing board meetings. The educational or spiritual value of members responding to each other is immense. It is through such informal interaction that members are supported in times of sorrow, are given help with ethical dilemmas, have friends with whom they celebrate important events, receive recognition as persons worthy of respect, and occasionally get help in their vocation. Probably such interaction communicates an interpretation of Christian beliefs and lifestyle more effectively than do formal Bible classes.[11]

LEARNING THROUGH EVENTS

The spontaneous interaction of church members is normally about their life situations or the church affairs in which they are involved. Sometimes an event happens that challenges members' beliefs and practices. At such a time conversation between members becomes focused on the event and how the congregation should respond. Every church member can remember such events because the learning was decisive for a real-life problem.

I will recall only one such event to illustrate how ethos functions as a teaching/learning process. When I was president of Louisville Presbyterian Seminary, a woman graduate, I'll call her Betty, became a candidate for an associate pastor position in a Presbyterian church in a large southern city. Betty was married. Her husband supported her vocation and his work allowed him to locate wherever she was called to be a pastor. She returned to the seminary after the interview with the pastor nominating committee feeling that things went well and she would be called to that position. A short time later she was notified by the committee's chairperson that she could not be called because a man on the committee said he was opposed to women pastors. Betty was surprised because she, and apparently members of the committee, did not know of this man's objection to women serving as pastors. Betty had started looking for other positions when, about a month later, she had a phone call from the chairperson of the committee saying the man had slowly come to the conclusion that he was wrong about women pastors. Having no question about Betty's qualifications, he was ready to vote for her. Betty, in talking to me about accepting the call under these conditions, finally decided to do so.

What happened to change this man's opposition to women pastors? We do not know. We believe that members of the committee talked to him, prayers for guidance were said, and the man was able to consider thoughtfully what people in the congregation thought about pastoral leadership. Since the event, including the man's change of mind, was well known in the congregation, it taught that women could serve as ministers, and people who were undecided about this matter learned why they should support women's rights to serve as pastors.

REFORMATION OF ETHOS

I consider the dynamic aspect of congregational life in neutral terms. The word "dynamic" simply describes the power that is generated as members interact with each other. This power could keep a congregation conservative, liberal, or club-like, as in the case of First Church in Windsor, Connecticut. Belonging to a congregation forms one's spiritual life because belonging influences a person to be like the group. Thus, the regular interaction of church members is a powerful form of education because it influences the perspective by which members interpret the Christian faith.

Since congregational dynamics describe a process rather than a product, the process can result in changing the ethos of a congregation. This may happen when an individual or a group embraces an idea about a belief or practice that should change. Change will not occur, however, if the idea is just a topic of conversation. Students of institutional life have formulated two principles about change that apply to congregations. One is that institutions can change when a group of people has a vision of the desired change and a dedication to work to make that vision a reality.[12] The other principle is that institutional changes most likely to endure are those that take place gradually so that people adopt them as their own. This principle of "disjointed incrementalism" means that leaders use events and situations as they occur to advance toward their vision rather than attempting to make important changes quickly.[13] Each small move toward the vision gets more people involved, which generates more support. Congregations are a voluntary association of people, so a vision that involves changes in members' convictions about the church's beliefs and practices is a serious educational venture. It involves church members' emotions as well as their reason. Thus, any significant change in a congregation's purpose or program will not endure unless an ever-increasing number of members affirm the change.

The Presbyterian Church in Mendocino, California, and the Church of the Covenant illustrate the two principles. The change in the Mendocino church started with the calling of a new pastor. Through his leadership of worship, sermons, pastoral work, and Bible classes, and his influence in the selection of officers, he was able in the course of a few years to move the majority of members from a liberal to a conservative interpretation of Christianity.

The odyssey of the Church of the Covenant started when three women became concerned about the welfare of political refugees from El Salvador. Through phone conversations with each other and friends, they gained enough influence to have a well-known Republican businessman speak about this concern at the church officers' retreat. They then started an adult class to discuss the political and religious aspects of sponsoring refugees. The congressman from their district led discussions, as well as historians and people who had various views about this matter. Through this adult class they enlarged the number of people who cared about helping the refugees. After a year of class discussion the congregation voted by a small majority to become a sanctuary church in defiance of government policy, and refugees were sponsored. The group, of which I was a member, that studied this congregation's struggle was impressed with the reaction of some members who voted against the proposal. Upon seeing the refugees, a well-respected leader who had opposed the proposal identified with the situation and offered them jobs.

The point to the above stories is not to glorify conflict. Rather it is to observe that differences of opinion in religious matters stimulate thinking and resolve; thus it is an important source of spiritual formation. Intense conflicts about beliefs that cause congregations to split apart are not desirable because they fracture the body of Christ. When splits do occur, people on each side of the controversy develop a heightened awareness of what they believe and a clearer understanding of what they are willing to defend and at what cost. There is probably no more powerful form of spiritual formation than that which takes place when people struggle to define the beliefs for which they are willing to stand firm.

The first question this chapter attempted to answer was, "How can we help church leaders become more aware of the natural processes of nurturing that occur in congregations?" My answer was to say that the ethos or spiritual character of a congregation is the most important element in its effort to nurture its members and children in the Christian faith. Ethos is communicated informally in conversations among members, casually by the lifestyles of members, and formally in worship, classes, policies, and programs sponsored by the church.

The second question was, "How can we use these processes more effectively?" My answer was for church leaders to gain a vision of what the church should be and work steadily toward that vision. This answer does not require new committees or programs, although such could emerge. Rather, this answer assumes that church leaders, especially ministers, become more concerned about the congregation having a well-defined mission. This goal is lacking in many mainstream congregations because, as noted at the beginning of this chapter, such congregations consist of many adults who are unclear about their beliefs. This situation is illustrated in the work of the Indianapolis Center for Congregations. This center is dedicated to helping congregations in the Indianapolis area identify their needs and providing resources to address those needs. After the first few years of consulting with leaders of many congregations, the director, John Wimmer, wrote that the most common need congregations voiced was, "We need to better understand our sense of mission and purpose as a congregation."[14] Some suggestions for helping congregations "to better understand" their mission are offered in the next two chapters.[15]

NOTES

[1] Quoted in Laurie Goodstein, "As Attacks' Impact Recedes, A Return to Religion as Usual," *New York Times*, late ed., 26 November 2001, Al. See also Robert Wuthnow, *Christianity and Civil Society* (Valley Forge PA: Trinity Press International, 1996), 21-26.

[2] Ernest Best, *One Body in Christ* (London: SPCK, 1955), 83-160.

[3] Carl S. Dudley, "Using Church Images for Commitment, Conflict, and Renewal," in *Congregations: Their Power to Form and Transform*, ed. C. Ellis Nelson (Louisville: Westminster/John Knox, 1988), 89-114.

[4] David A. Roozen, William McKinney, and Jackson W. Carroll, *Varieties of Religious Presence* (New York: Pilgrim Press, 1984).

[5] Don S. Browning, *A Fundamental Practical Theology* (Minneapolis: Fortress Press, 1991), 26-33.

[6] Nelle G. Slater, ed., *Tensions Between Citizenship and Discipleship* (New York: Pilgrim Press, 1989), 1-27. My essay in Slater's book, "Some Educational Aspects of Conflict," discusses some of the dynamics of the power struggle in this congregation. See pp. 195-218.

[7] R. Stephen Warner, *New Wine in Old Wineskins* (Berkeley: University of California Press, 1990).

[8] Gary Dorsey, *Congregation* (New York: Penguin Books, 1995), 345.

[9] Penny Edgell Becker, *Congregations in Conflict* (New York: Cambridge University Press, 1999).

[10] Nile Harper, *Urban Churches, Vital Signs* (Grand Rapids: Wm. B. Eerdmans Publishers, 1999).

[11] Charles R. Foster, "Communicating: Informal Conversation in the Congregation's Education," in *Congregations: Their Power to Form and Transform*, ed. C. Ellis Nelson (Louisville: Westminster/John Knox, 1988), 218-38.

[12] Robert A. Dahl, *A Preface to Democratic Theory* (Chicago: University of Chicago Press, 1956), 132.

[13] David Braybrooke and Charles E. Lindblom, *A Strategy of Decision* (New York: Free Press, 1963), 61-79.

[14] John Wimmer, "Listening to Parish Leaders: Clarifying the Issues," *Congregations*, May-June 1998, 9.

[15] See Jeffrey D. Jones, *Traveling Together* (Herndon VA: Alban Institute Press, 2006) for additional suggestions about how a congregation may focus its life on the formation of disciples.

Chapter 6

FORMAL PROCESSES OF NURTURING:

WORSHIP AND SERMON

Informal and formal processes of nurturing are closely related in liberal or conservative congregations. In these churches leaders clearly define beliefs and a lifestyle based on those beliefs. Church leaders carefully select teachers, interest group leaders, officers, and, in many cases, employees who share their interpretations of Christianity.

Mainstream Protestant congregations consist, according to Wuthnow's analysis, of "devout" and "mildly interested" people. As a result there are varieties of beliefs about God in these congregations, and about the only attempt to advocate an approved lifestyle is through sermons and classroom instruction. The problem, therefore, is how church leaders, in addition to using informal processes, can use formal processes of nurture to help church members gain a clearer understanding of Christian beliefs and become more concerned about forming their lives in accord with those beliefs.

BELIEFS AND LIFESTYLE

The solution to this problem is for members of a congregation to *experience* the meaning of Christian beliefs. Denominations have creeds that have been refined over hundreds of years. These creeds that are used in worship, sermons, and classroom instruction define major beliefs about God and humankind. The question is, "What meaning do church members give to these theological statements?" or "How do members experience the Christian beliefs they hear and recite?" The Apostles' Creed, for example, is recited in churches throughout the world. Church members repeat, "I believe . . . in the forgiveness of sins" and assume correctly that God may forgive their sins. Yet in the same worship service members may repeat in the Lord's Prayer, "And forgive us our debts, as we also have forgiven our debtors," without believing that Jesus said God's forgiveness was dependent on their forgiving others (Matt 6:12, 14-15). Congregations may follow the worship ritual of their denomination based on traditional beliefs that include a confession of sins yet do little or nothing about conditions in their community about which they have prayed. Congregations sometimes build steeples taller than any in town, order an organ grander than any other church's organ, or in other ways drift into prideful statements that are not in harmony with their creedal statements.

The gap between formal statements of Christian beliefs and the beliefs by which individuals live is a human situation described throughout the Bible. We are acquainted with the way Old Testament prophets, especially Hosea, Amos, and Micah, identified the gap between the concerns of God and the way God's people lived. Jesus continued this observation by saying to the crowds and to his disciples, "The scribes and the Pharisees sit on Moses' seat; therefore, do whatever they teach you and follow it; but do not do as they do, for they do not practice what they teach" (Matt 23:1-3).

I have been helped in dealing with this gap by John E. Smith, a philosopher who considers experience to be the bridge between belief and practice. Smith honors rational efforts to comprehend God, but he is unwilling to allow reason to be the major source of our knowledge of God. His thesis is, "merely knowing that a doctrine has a certain conceptual content and merely holding doctrines are not enough; there remains the actual undergoing of the experience to which the doctrine points."[1] From a historical perspective, Smith contends that the reformers, Luther and Calvin, rejected medieval theology's analytical detachment from human experience and the Catholic Church's cycle of contrition and penance. The reformers insisted that one becomes right with God through faith in God that is confirmed by one's experience.[2] Luther's struggle for justification is well known. His decision to become a monk was prompted by his experience in a thunderstorm during which he was thrown to the ground. His early life as a monk was characterized by a study of the Bible and an intense desire to understand how he could be acceptable to God. Slowly his meditation on Romans 1:17, "The one who is righteous will live by faith," led him to experience God as gracious, to challenge the value of indulgences, and to reformulate church life.[3]

Calvin's theology is characterized by its clarity, comprehensiveness, and rationality. His emphasis on living by Christian moral standards is often considered legalistic and harsh. If, however, one observes Calvin as a pastor and teacher, one will find him, like the other reformers, wanting people to experience God as a reality that guides their personal lives. This aspect of Calvin's theology is displayed in his reply to Cardinal Sadolet's letter to the Senate and People of Geneva (1539). Cardinal Sadolet's letter was written to encourage the people of Geneva to return to the Roman Catholic Church. Calvin's reply goes directly to doctrines, such as justification by faith, and describes how he as a pastor taught the catechism.

> First, we bid a man begin by examining himself, and this not in a superficial and perfunctory manner, but to present his conscience before the tribunal of God and, when sufficiently convinced of his iniquity, to reflect on the strictness of the sentence pronounced upon all sinners. Thus confounded and stricken with misery, he is prostrated and humbled before God; and, throwing away all self-confidence, he groans as though given up to final perdition. Then we show that the only haven of safety is in the mercy of God as manifested in Christ, in whom every part of our salvation is completed. . . . We maintain that in this way man is reconciled in Christ to God the Father, by no merit of his own, by no worthiness of works, but by gratuitous mercy. When we embrace Christ by faith and come, as it were, into communion with him, we term this in the manner of Scripture the righteousness of faith.[4]

Unfortunately, the view of Luther, Calvin, and other Reformers that beliefs and experience were two parts of the one way to understand God did not become firmly established. As the Reformation spread throughout Western Europe, Protestants tended to emphasize their differences with the Catholic Church on doctrinal grounds. Since doctrines were the basis of Protestant distinctiveness, many Protestants, especially Calvinists, used doctrinal statements as the test of true Christianity, with less attention to practicing what the beliefs required. There are several reasons for this situation. One is mental: our ability to think that if we can state Christian beliefs correctly we have experienced what they mean. Another is psychological (well stated by Paul): "For I do not do the good I want, but the evil I do not want is what I do" (Rom 7:19).

As a practical matter, the gap between beliefs and a Christian lifestyle in mainstream Protestant congregations is well known. Sermons, Bible readings, and classes constantly remind us of this deficiency. What is lacking is help in relating life experience to Christian beliefs. This lack may be due to finding time for adults to discuss their religious experience, to the reluctance of church members to talk about their personal situations, to group leaders' feelings of inadequacy about leading a discussion of people's personal faith convictions, or to the idea that the church should simply proclaim the truth about God and expect members to apply the truth to their personal lives. All of these reasons have some validity, but if a congregation is going to help members become "mature in Christ," there are ways to help church members relate their life experiences to their beliefs.

Before offering some suggestions about bridging this gap, it is important that I note that Jesus was always identified as a teacher by his disciples, by ordinary people, and by his enemies. Jesus' method of teaching was most often in the form of a conversation. By this means Jesus engaged the attitudes, values, and mental processes of the people to whom he was speaking. At times Jesus started with beliefs and then moved to the experience a person should have as he did with the rich young ruler (Matt 19:16-26), or as in the parable of the Good Samaritan (Luke 10:29-37). At other times Jesus started with a lifestyle problem and moved to a belief the people should understand, as he did with Sabbath observance (Matt 12:9-14) or life after death (Luke 20:27-40).

The following suggestions are offered as examples of how mainstream Protestant congregations could use their formal processes to enhance their efforts to relate beliefs to practice. The suggestions are practical, but they should not be considered applicable to all churches. What has worked well in one congregation may not be feasible in another.

LEADERSHIP

This congregational model of nurture works with a pattern of influence. It assumes the congregation as a "fellowship of kindred minds" is the most influential agency for defining Christian beliefs and practice. Normally the congregation's mission is established, maintained, or changed by its pastors and governing board. Pastors, being the recognized leaders of the congregation, are the persons who normally take the initiative for defining and suggesting ways to accomplish the church's mission. Thus pastors are always in a teaching mode when they meet with the governing board. How pastors play this role is of critical importance. One pastor might include a brief study of the Bible or a section of the church's creed as a part of each governing board meeting. Another pastor may schedule retreats for a day or two for the governing board to review its work in light of the congregation's mission. Regardless of method, some formal, prayerful study of the church's faith is necessary in order that the governing board remembers that all of the decisions it makes for the congregation are an incarnation of the board's beliefs. Decisions such as the use of church property, projects approved for support, job descriptions of and policies concerning staff positions, and actions related to other denominations and religions become observable characteristics of the congregation. Perhaps the most accurate indication of what a congregation considers important is its budget. Each budget item, seen in relation to the total budget, is probably a better indication of what the majority of board members believe about God than is their theological creed.

Because church officers are selected from the pool of most active members and because this pool of prospective officers is often composed of group leaders or teachers, I suggest that pastors teach a Central Study Group. The purpose is to develop a practical theology for the officers as well as a Christian mentality for members to help them have clearer theological reasons for daily decision-making. Through this Central Study Group, pastors can extend their vision of what the congregation should be and could do. Practical problems for the study group include the selection of people, when and where to meet, and duration of the study. These problems can be solved if pastors see such a group as a way to develop a shared vision of congregational life and to build support for it.[5]

The idea of pastors teaching a Central Study Group came to me a few years ago when I was teaching an adult class in a church. While there I learned that the minister—I'll name him Bill Goodenough— taught an unadvertised Bible class for adults at the Sunday school hour. In conversation with Goodenough, I learned that he started the class soon after he became pastor. He did so because, he said, "I like to teach the Bible," and he wanted to know the officers and their spouses. The class was unadvertised because he did not want to disrupt the established classes for adults, and he limited the class to twenty persons, the number that would fit in his study. The small number in a crowded room made for an informal, discussion-type setting. The class met for one year, then a new class was formed. When I talked with Goodenough about his class, he had been pastor of this church of about 650 members for seven years. Thus, 140 officers, teachers, and most active adult members of the church had spent a year sharing biblical interpretation with their pastor. I asked Goodenough toward the end of our conversation if he taught this class as a strategy for influencing the congregation. He seemed surprised and said, "I just like to teach the Bible, and I wanted to get acquainted with the religious beliefs of most active members of the congregation." The unintended consequence of his class was a congregation that, from my perspective as an outsider, was serious about its commitment to be a Christian church.

There are many ways a vision or mission of a congregation can be formulated, but the mission will not become a motivating factor unless a significant number of members share it. In addition to classes and informal methods of spiritual formation for officers, congregations nurture members in a formal, direct way in worship and through instruction (covered in chapter 7).

WORSHIP

Worship is our response to who God is as revealed in the Bible and Jesus Christ—our guardian, guide, and redeemer. Our response is glorification of God in a spirit of gratitude. In worship we focus on God, not each other. Yet what people do together in worship is a powerful form of persuasion and a direct form of teaching. The building, furnishings, decorations, music, hymns, prayers, Scripture readings, announcements, celebration of sacraments, and sermon all express mental images of God and our relation to God. Moreover, for church members, the major events of life—baptism, confirmation of faith in Christ, marriage, and death—are all celebrated in the context of worship. Although each element of worship is directly related to God and what God expects of us, I will comment only on music, sermon, and testimonial thanksgiving.

Music

Music communicates directly to one's inner self—the soul. We frequently have mystical feelings that cannot be adequately expressed in words. When music is coordinated with poetic language in hymns, we experience a presence of God that is intensely real. Thus the singing of hymns in worship has the possibility of reaching and strengthening the feelings that underlie Christian characteristics such as love, joy, peace, longsuffering, gentleness, goodness, hope, and faith (Gal 5:22; Rom 15:13).

Sermon

In mainstream Protestant churches, the sermon is considered the most direct effort to inspire and instruct believers. Pastors, trained in Bible, theology, and church history and sensitive to the spiritual situation of the congregation, select sermon topics they consider important for the church they serve. Thus a sermon's message is what the pastor thinks the members should learn. It can be properly termed "curriculum"—what the church members should know, understand, and use in their Christian life.

Although sermons are delivered to the congregation, they are addressed to individuals, and this is their greatest value. Individuals come to worship with a set of general interests as well as personal concerns or problems. The Scripture/sermon element in worship often speaks directly to hearers' interests or concerns, thus helping those persons connect their life experience with Christian beliefs. Others, hearing the same sermon, may not make a connection with their life situation so the message is soon forgotten. Because sermons have endured as a part of worship since biblical times as a significant way to maintain and interpret the Christian faith and because sermons continue to confirm church members' faith in

God, the issue is how to make the sermon applicable to a larger number of hearers.

The principle by which sermons can become important to more members is to process their exposition and admonition by discussion in small groups. All of us have experienced the value of discussing chapters, movies, plays, or current events with a group of friends. Because adults or older teenagers bring to the sermon discussion their interests, experience, education, and beliefs about God, such conversations clarify the meaning of the sermon and reveal the ways individuals connect it to their life situation. If the church scheduled classes after a worship service, members could come with notes taken during the sermon. Many ministers know days or weeks in advance the Scripture to be used and the topic of a Sunday's sermon. In such cases the class leader could study the biblical passage and e-mail the passage to class members in advance. Some ministers make their sermons available in printed or audiotape form a week after they are preached. Using a printed text would facilitate a group's discussion because members could focus on a passage as they respond to it.

While attending a church in Louisville, Kentucky, I observed a unique way for a pastor to relate his sermon to the felt needs of the congregation. The pastor, Tom McClure, arranged with the youth group that once a month he would preach on whatever topic or concern the group proposed, provided it was also of interest to the whole congregation. On Sunday night he would meet with the youth group to discuss the sermon. The first Sunday this plan went into operation, McClure's sermon was on "How to Know the Will of God." The teenagers occupied the front rows of the sanctuary and took notes. The teenagers had spent several of their Sunday night meetings selecting this topic because they were concerned about their vocational choice. They thought that if God had any meaning for their lives it would certainly be about their life's work. Parents of the teenagers as well as others in the congregation could also relate to that topic in their decision-making.

I saw a different way to connect the sermon with experiences members of the congregation were having in Tenafly, New Jersey. The pastor, who also conducted the confirmation class, announced that next Sunday's sermon would be on sin and he would use ideas teenagers had offered during their confirmation class. The teenagers were present as he compared their language about sin with biblical and theological statements. I was impressed with their vivid language about sin and with their personal struggle to maintain their values while some of their school pals were testing the limits of moral and legal behavior.

Michael Warren, writing from a Roman Catholic perspective, affirmed the reforms in worship approved by Vatican Council II. He notes, however, that the term "liturgical assembly" implies that the people gathered for worship are more than an audience. The word "assembly" suggests that although the people may respond to various parts of the service, there is no provision for participation in the sermon. Warren understands any effort to include the people assembled for worship in a dialogue with the priest about the homily would be extremely difficult. How would a congregation decide to have such a dialogue? What method of dialogue would be used? What consideration should be given to the people who do not want to participate? In spite of these and other problems, Warren asked himself:

> [W]hat would shift in the conditions of speech in worship if at the end of the service, the readings for the following week were announced or even distributed and worshipers agreed to reflect and pray over these readings during the week, in preparation for the following week's assembly? Then during the next assembly, after the reading of these texts, the assembly—at least those wishing to do so—would break into small groups of three or four and listen briefly to one another's responses to these readings. Such a procedure would signal that all can speak, that all can respond to the Word of God, that all can learn from all, that the Word of God is on the lips of the people. After this sharing, the presider could invite a certain number of persons to tell of some insight heard from another so that the group would have some sense of common and uncommon issues. Finally, the presider might make a very brief comment summarizing some feature of the insights from the floor. What might in the beginning be a somewhat messy procedure might in the end find the Word of God alive within the assembly.[6]

The possibility of mainstream Protestant congregations following Warren's suggestion is not very good. Protestants are so accustomed to preaching as proclamation to which they respond individually that change is hardly possible. The role of the minister as pastor, leader of the congregation trained in Bible and theology, counselor and friend causes members to refrain from any but favorable responses to sermons. Also, psychologically, members may prefer to respond to sermons privately for then they can accept what they like and find reasons to reject what does not suit them. For example, I have attended Presbyterian churches where the minister invited members to stay after church to discuss the sermon, but few did. I attended a church in California where a nationally known preacher was pastor. He invited members to meet with him on Wednesday nights to discuss the biblical passage on which he would preach the following Sunday, but only six or eight people from a large congregation responded.

If we are concerned to help a larger number of people understand the sermon as the pastor's effort to coach the congregation through its members to be mature "in Christ," then we should study it for that purpose. As a general rule to which there may be exceptions, such as the account of the pastor of the church in Louisville, I recommend that sermon discussions be led by laypersons in groups of about ten to twenty. The leader should focus the comments on what the sermon means to individuals and to the life and work of the congregation. Although the leader may summarize the discussion at the end of class time, there should be no effort to forge conclusions. Individuals should feel at the end of the discussion that they have a better understanding of the sermon and a clearer sense of how it relates to their life situations.

Experience-centered Thanksgiving

Ministers often use religious experience, their own and others', to illustrate their sermons. Where this is done to show the connection between human events and beliefs about God, it is usually this part of the sermon that is remembered. How to arrange for church members to share in a worship setting their experiences that relate an event to Christian beliefs is so difficult that it is seldom attempted.

Lee Bowman, a Presbyterian minister in Austin, Texas, developed an excellent way to deal with the problem. She used the thanksgiving worship service as a time for three or four church members to speak to the congregation about their thankfulness to God for guidance in a recent event in their lives. The statements were recorded, transcribed, and made available the next Sunday. Thus, church members' testimonies about their relationships with God were available along with the pastor's sermons for the spiritual edification of all members. From the thirty or more testimonies available, I selected two as examples of how experience was the bridge between beliefs and life's events.

One was the story of a modern prodigal son. Although raised in a fine Presbyterian family, his young adult years were spent with the attitude, "If it feels good, I tried it." After drifting through two marriages, he finally had no money. When his father died, he came to himself. With the help of a new wife and the ministry of many church members, he has come to realize that he *is* in the process of growing up spiritually. He concluded his story with the following self-analysis.

In the years since the death of my dad I have experienced what I would like to think of as spiritual maturity. I have come to realize that God's promise fulfilled is spiritual maturity. This has not come to me in some great revelation like I always thought it would. Rather, it is more like when you stand next to a fire. At first it warms your outside a little bit and as you stand there that warmth spreads throughout your whole being, it encompasses your whole soul. That is what it has been like for me.

God speaks to us in many ways and in many voices. Sometimes that voice is very soft and quiet—so you have to listen very carefully. Let me give you an example. When I was preparing for this Sunday I went for a walk. I find that I often hear God's voice in nature. As I was walking, trying to clear my mind, so that I could hear God's voice, I noticed an oak tree. On that tree there were two wounds where the branches had been removed. One I had treated with wound-dressing and the other I had missed and it had gone untreated. The wound that had been cared for was healing over, while the untreated was not and was being invaded by insects. To me, this was God saying to me that there are still things in my life that I need to work on—wounds that still need healing. With God's help, through Jesus Christ, I can do it.

The second story is from a woman who is an active member of her church. I will quote the full text of her story because it illustrates how a mature Christian woman found an area of her life that needed attention. With the help of her pastor and friends in the congregation, she apprehended Jesus' teaching about forgiveness.

I consider it a privilege to be able to share with you this morning a recent story of God's grace in my own life. My story begins two years ago in the springtime when my younger daughter, Sara, announced her engagement. It was happy news for all of us, for we had seen Sara and Richard meet in their college days. We watched the romance bloom and deepen. Everyone felt it was a good match. Looking ahead, it meant that we would have a full year to make plans for the wedding and celebrate. Sara would be coming home and spending the last month with us all, and that was very good news. It also meant that I would be interacting with my ex-husband, Ralph, from whom I had been divorced eleven years. But, I didn't see that as any problem. Ralph and I had had an amicable divorce and had remained friends. We had made a commitment when our marriage dissolved that we would keep our children as our number one priority and they prospered under that commitment. I had just read a book called *Dance of Intimacy* by [Harriet] Lerner, and in it she writes that if anyone has any unfinished emotional business, a wedding or a funeral will certainly kick it up. I didn't think, though, that applied to me. The only difficulty I could see was there might be some financial negotiations that even with strong, healthy marriages are sometimes strained by a wedding.

People even described Ralph and me as a happily divorced couple. He had come to me after the divorce and sought forgiveness and I had said the words. Through the decade there had been other opportunities for more forgiveness. I got pretty good at it.

I even began to like it. I began to even tell my story. I went on church lay-renewals and told how I had forgiven him. I began to wear my story like a peacock. I embellished it to add more feathers to the plumage.

Well, the only possible difficulty probably would be money. Spring turned to early fall and it became time to make serious preparations and decisions—and the parents hit a snag, our first

disagreement. The irony is, I don't even remember what that disagreement was, but what I do remember is the strange woman who
exploded out of me, raging with resentment, anger, and dark hate.
That woman made Sara cry on the telephone in Atlanta. I was
stunned. I had never caused either of my daughters to cry. I felt
horrified and frightened and ashamed because I saw in myself the
result of pure concentrated hatred that had settled to the bottom of
my very being during those years. What I also saw clearly for the
first time was a woman who had not forgiven Ralph; even worse,
she did not want to.

In the fall, our minister gave a series of sermons about women.
For those of you who heard them, he told a story of a woman in
Luke 13 who was bent over emotionally for eighteen years. That
story really gripped me because I saw inside myself a woman who
had been bent over emotionally almost just as long. Immediately I
sought ministerial help here at our church. It was the month of
September. Over the course of several months I received pastoral
guidance—sensitive, spiritual help, loving and tender kindness, an
outpouring of prayer and an extraordinary reminder that Jesus was
with me. A reminder that He, too, had known disappointment,
pain, betrayal, sorrow, even death. For the first time I was asked to
look at my shortcomings in the sixteen years of marriage. In all the
professional counseling I had received, no one had ever asked me
to do that because the arrow of blame seemed to point so clearly in
the other direction. It was difficult work. I was asked to get in
touch with the hate that I felt—to visualize it, to find an image of
it. At the time that seemed like a painful and terrifying experience.
I was assured that this was a gift. *"A gift?!"* I said. This didn't seem
like my idea of a gift! I was assured that marriage was the gift for
Sara and Richard, but my gift was finally a chance for forgiveness.

I worked hard to dry out those tears and the memory of them
on beloved Sara's cheeks. She had said to me over the phone,
"Mom, I love my daddy. I am trying to have a relationship with
him and you keep tearing him down." I took a whole day and set it
aside to spend in prayer and solitude to face my own shortcomings. To my surprise, they poured out and I surrendered pages and
pages of writings about my failings. I faced inequities that were not
only from the past, but wrong living in the present. Tough decisions were made to change course as it became clear that the only
path I could follow is the one that led to God. Prayer filled the void
as the anger, black as soot, bellowed out of me, while peace and
forgiveness poured in and I felt the Lord's gentle hand. God's grace

embraced me. On December 1 I called Ralph and I asked him to come for breakfast. I made oatmeal in the kitchen and muffins and coffee and we sat on the kitchen stools the way we had many years before. I asked him not to say anything and not to respond, but to listen and I apologized to him for my failings in the marriage. We decided for Christmas we would give our children an apology for the break-up of our family.

The forgiveness session was extraordinary. The light on Ralph's face lit the entire house. I hadn't thought about his response. It was an unexpected gift. The four of us came here on Christmas Eve for Communion to give thanks. I looked up the definition of grace. In the New Testament the word "grace" refers to the unmerited and freely given redeeming action of God through Christ by which sin is forgiven and its power broken and believers are upheld and strengthened in their Christian life.

I understand and believe in God's grace. Though my own marriage is dissolved and my family is grown and gone, I have been upheld and strengthened in my Christian life through an extraordinary family here at our church. Ministers, staff, teachers, lay-leaders, many, many members and friends have been a very important part of my spiritual growth and my own healing—for that I feel extremely blessed.

Well, the wedding was perfect. The parents danced and laughed together. I've never known such concentrated joy. There were a couple of tough negotiations after it was all over, but the power of God's love has prevailed. This year, the day after Valentine's, Ralph and I both received a call from our older daughter, Kristine, announcing her engagement. A couple of weeks ago we had lunch together with an old couple friend and we talked about how lucky we are to be having another happy event for 1992.

Through this experience I have learned that emotional healing can take a long time, and sometimes a lot of personal and professional work and a lot of prayer and worship, but no matter where we are, God loves us. I have a new understanding of the words of the Lord's prayer, "forgive us our debts as we forgive our debtors." I now stand in awe more than ever and wonder at God's majesty and divine ability to transform lives. I feel like that bent-over woman when Jesus said to her, "Woman, you are freed from your sickness." Today, I stand fully erect and tall on the inside as well as the outside and with a deeper faith say . . . thanks and glory be to God. Amen.

Listening to church members testify to their congregation, including family and friends, about how Christian beliefs relate to their life experience is probably the most powerful form of instruction. There are, however, serious problems with this process of Christian nurture. Some adults may make up or exacerbate the details of their story to gain sympathy from the congregation. Some adults may be more concerned about their experience than they are about Christian beliefs. Some may have a valuable story but not be able to compose it into a coherent presentation. Then there are some adults who have such an immature idea of God that their story would not help members of the congregation. Lee Bowman's way of solving these problems was to lead a class on spiritual formation. Members of this class were learning how to relate their life experience to Christian beliefs. Bowman was able to select from the class persons with a story that conformed to Paul's rules for speaking to the congregation. Paul wrote that speaking to the church should be for spiritual "upbuilding and encouragement and consolation" (1 Cor 14:3).[7]

NOTES

[1] John E. Smith, *The Analogy of Experience* (New York: Harper & Row, 1973), 28-29.

[2] Ibid., 26-27. See also Smith's *Experience and God* (New York: Oxford University Press, 1968) for an extended philosophical discussion of this point.

[3] Walther von Loewenich, *Martin Luther: The Man and His Work* (Minneapolis: Augsburg Publishing House, 1986), 54, 7-105.

[4] *Calvin: Theological Treatises*, trans. J. K. S. Reid, *The Library of Christian Classics*, vol. 22 (Philadelphia: Westminster Press, 1954), 234-35.

[5] C. Ellis Nelson, *How Faith Matures* (Louisville: Westminster/John Knox Press, 1989), 204-13.

[6] Michael Warren, *At This Time in This Place* (Harrisburg PA: Trinity Press International, 1999), 88.

[7] Although church members testifying about what their faith means to them in a specific life situation has a long history, such sharing of religious experience has seldom been a part of mainstream Protestant churches in recent times. A full discussion of the importance of personal testimony has been written by Lillian Daniel in her book *Tell It Like It Is* (Herndon VA: Alban Institute Press, 2005).

Chapter 7

FORMAL PROCESSES OF NURTURING:

INSTRUCTION

Instruction, as featured in the previous chapter, takes place in every aspect of worship. I selected the Scripture/sermon element in worship for special comment because it contains beliefs and practices individuals should connect with their life situation. The other elements in worship such as prayer, creeds, and hymns should also be studied and related to worshipers' concerns. Since these aspects of worship are used every Sunday, perhaps they should be a part of the regular instructional program for adults.

Systematic instruction has always been a part of Christian history.[1] This congregational strategy of Christian nurture continues that tradition. Agencies of Christian education such as the Sunday school, church-sponsored camps and conferences, retreats, weekday childcare, Vacation Bible Schools, and church-related colleges that emerged during the 1800s and 1900s continue to have a place in the formation of Christians. In addition to systematic instruction, these agencies provide fellowship with peers in a classroom and social setting that can be, and often is, an excellent sharing of Christian values. We must continue these agencies of education as long as they respond to a need in the formation of Christian beliefs and practices.

What is the difference in this congregational strategy of Christian nurture and our traditional Protestant model? In general terms, the answer is American culture, which, although historically a product of religious values, is now so infused with secular values that it no longer can be expected to communicate the beliefs about God that formed our social values. Congregations today must become more concerned about identifying and explaining Christian beliefs because what people actually believe forms their lifestyle. In practical terms, congregational life generates a pattern of influence in the following priority order:

1. The ethos of the congregation as expressed and celebrated in worship is the primary source of influence. Chapter 4 illustrated the role of beliefs in the life of a congregation. Chapter 5 explained how informal processes that go on continuously in a congregation are powerful forms of nurture. Chapter 6 was devoted to the educational aspect of worship and suggested ways the Scripture/sermon can engage a larger number of members.
2. Next to worship, the systematic instruction of adults is the most significant influence for the spiritual growth of Christians. This is because adults, in concert with the pastor, make decisions that form the congregation's beliefs and expected lifestyle. Adults are the leaders of groups and teachers of the church's classes. Also, adults in their workplaces are in a position to have some influence on culture.
3. Family life is the most important religious influence for children. Parents and children's caregivers are the first teachers of religion. As I described in chapters 2 and 3, children form their earliest images of God from their relationships with parents. Parents do a lot of direct teaching about God and what God expects of children as they answer children's questions. Thus the congregation's first ministry to children is to help parents maintain a Christian family.
4. Church agencies for the Christian education of children and teenagers support and enlarge upon what they are learning at home by systematic study and by participation in the life and work of the congregation.

Warning: Do not assume that these four ways of nurturing church members stand alone. On the contrary, each of the four is in constant interaction with the other three through the people who are involved to some degree with all of them. What is at issue is the order of priority. Although this congregational strategy is based on the pattern of influence, it is difficult to use. Suggestions for dealing with the difficulties will be discussed in the following sections on adult instruction, parents instructing children, and church instruction of children and youth.

CHURCH INSTRUCTION OF ADULTS

Adult education is the first instructional priority because of adults' influence in the congregation, the family, and all of their social relations. Shifting from a child/youth educational priority, used by most Protestant congregations, to placing adult education first is difficult for the following reasons:

- Since the 1800s Protestants have invested energy and financial resources in Sunday schools and various group activities for children and youth. This tradition is hard to change because American culture supports the idea that whatever we want children to learn is taught in a school.
- Many parents feel they have discharged their duty for the religious and moral education of their children by sending them to a Sunday school. Thinking instruction is for children and youth, these parents do not attend classes for adults.
- Some adults will not attend classes for adults because they believe they already know all that is important about Christianity.
- Some adults avoid classes because the teacher is boring or because they do not like to participate in discussions.
- Many adults are so involved in work outside the home, with family responsibilities, and with sports that they have no time for study or to attend classes. These adults consider attendance at worship and perhaps a few church activities where they are a part of the audience adequate for their religious life.
- Some adults fear that a careful study of the Bible or theology will pressure them to change their lifestyle, something they do not intend to do.
- Adults who think that only the pastors or staff people who have formal theological training are competent to teach will not attend classes taught by others.

These and other reasons make systematic instruction of adults difficult to sustain in typical Protestant congregations.[2] If, however, we take seriously the corroding nature of contemporary American culture and the influence adults have in the areas they control—congregations and family—then we must attend to the goal that they "grow in the grace and knowledge of our Lord and Savior Jesus Christ" (2 Pet 3:18).

You may have noticed that the list of difficulties did not include curriculum. All of our mainstream denominations publish excellent study materials for adults. In addition, Lutheran, Presbyterian, and Methodist church leaders have prepared excellent long-term studies of the whole Bible, which require a significant investment of study time.[3] The success of these programs proves there are a large number of adults in our churches who want a serious, systematic study of the Bible. Also, for almost every topic in Christian theology there is a book for laypeople to study. The issues that congregations need to resolve in order for most adult members to become more mature in their faith are practical, motivational, and educational.

Practical

Planning an adult Christian education program is different from the planning we do for children and youth. Christian education must be planned *with* adults, for they are in charge of their lives and they have influence in the life and work of the congregation. This means planning should proceed slowly and involve as many adults as possible, and, in most situations, as many as possible of the established classes or activity groups should be continued. Developing an enduring adult Christian education program that reaches a high percent of the adult members and inspires them to identify and "put an end to" their childish ideas of God will never be achieved, but progress toward that goal can be made.

Ministers, directors of Christian education, and church leaders must consider every aspect of the congregation's situation when they plan and manage an instructional program with adults. Each congregation has a history, characteristics, needs, and a limited number of available teachers or group leaders. In addition to these factors, the size of the congregation is an important consideration. Leaders of a small church with one pastor may decide that worship, frequent courses by the minister, and a ministry to parents to help them with home nurture of children is a satisfactory instructional program for adults.

Congregations with pastors and staff persons trained in Christian education have many options for adult education, but they also have the problem of selecting topics for instruction and teachers capable of leading adults into a more mature faith. Often church leaders will distribute a list of topics for adults to check the ones in which they are interested. Although this is a useful way to identify concerns, such surveys do not always indicate what church members really need. If, however, the checklist clusters a lot of votes for certain topics, it is important to find out why people share this interest. Conversations with a representative group of people who checked a certain topic are necessary to find out what lies behind their preference. Such conversations may lead to a theme that was not apparent. I prefer that adult Christian education be primarily Bible study or about theological/ethical themes. These are the areas of study that can help form a mature faith in God.

Motivation

Many of the difficulties of adult Christian education mentioned earlier are related to motivation. Some church leaders tend to overcome adults' resistance to study by using guilt or shame, saying, "You ought to study the Bible," or "You need to know more about theology." Rather than using these or other psychological ploys to gain attendance, I recommend we interest adults in learning more about how they relate to God by explaining the importance of that relationship. Church members have some understanding of God. The motive, building on that commitment, should be to identify and put away our childish images of God as we strive to become more mature in our Christian faith. The following list provides some places in the life of a congregation where instruction of adults has a built-in motivation.

Adult Communicants Class. Adults who join a church on their profession of faith in Christ are open to instruction. Congregations should have a course designed to cover their major theological beliefs. If the number of people who join a congregation by profession of faith at one time is small, the materials prepared for the class should be individually studied by the prospective members and discussed with the pastor. Although the adult communicants class covers basic Christian beliefs, new members should be encouraged to join an adult class that will enlarge their knowledge and understanding of the Christian faith.

New Members. Adults who join a congregation by transferring their membership from another church are often given a warm welcome and literature about the congregation's programs. Since joining a congregation is a new beginning, it is an opportunity to include in the welcome an expectation that they become part of a study group. Some congregations provide a sponsor for each new member who for months introduces them informally before and after worship and who helps them select a study group.

Officers. In their role as decision-makers for the congregation, officers become spokespersons for its beliefs and models of an expected lifestyle. If ministers have time for but one teaching responsibility beyond the adult communicants class, it should be with the officers. Although education of officers can be done in retreats or in a series of special classes, the most convenient time and place is during regular scheduled meetings. If thirty minutes were allocated for study at each meeting, a pastor could cover a considerable part of the Bible or theology of the church in a few years.

Parents. The adults most motivated to learn are parents. Because the home as an agency of Christian nurture is so important, it will be discussed in the next section.

Parts of Worship. Members of mainstream Protestant churches quickly become accustomed to the order of worship and commit to memory the parts they recite. This does not mean that church members understand the parts of worship or the reasons why elements such as a confession of sin are included. Being participants in worship means they have some motivation to examine what they are doing in worship and why they continue to do so. Such a study should include a careful discussion of each part of the liturgy, including the music and theology in the hymns sung most frequently.

Lure of Learning. In addition to the motivation associated with situations already noted, there is the lure of learning. Seldom do we find church members who are proud of their ignorance about their religion. The issue is the kind of learning offered to adults. Since attendance is optional, courses should be about matters to which adults can connect their beliefs and practice. Courses on church history, world religions, or theology are an important part of adult Christian education if teachers connect the information with contemporary life. This does not mean that all adult courses must be practical or useful, but what is taught should be worth learning for adults to grow in their faith.

Formal instruction normally takes place in a classroom on a set schedule. A teaching/learning process takes place, but the two are easily separated. Teachers come to class with ideas, information, feelings, attitudes, and values they want students to understand and appreciate. Some students may learn all the teacher wants to communicate. Some students may acquire the knowledge but come to dislike the subject. Other students may learn to love the subject and decide to take more courses but not from this teacher. Because the educational process is a human enterprise, the results are difficult to anticipate. This is especially characteristic of the teaching of religion because religion is about beliefs for which there are no factual data. The only observable effects of religious faith are in a person's speech and behavior. We can, however, make formal instruction of adults more effective if we commit to the following steps:[5] (1) Attend to the desired outcome. (2) Have teachers coaching adults to experience faith in God.

Step 1: Attend to the desired outcome. The outcome of adult Christian education is for church members to learn how to identify and "put an end to" their childish images of God as they turn their attention to what God expects of them. This goal is probably impossible to reach, but it serves to guide the special nature of Christian education.

This expectation of change in the lives of adults means that knowledge of church history, theology, or the Bible is necessary but not sufficient for the Christian life. In chapter 3 I used the story of Charles Colson and Millard Fuller as examples of how church members made a dramatic change in their lives when events forced them to ask, "What does God desire of me?" In chapter 4 I listed many of the things Paul "put an end to" after his conversion because I wanted to illustrate how his three years with a Christian congregation nurtured his change in character. I could have used Peter's story because, according to the book of Acts, he was the recognized leader of the disciples after the resurrection. He is always named first in the listing of disciples. He is credited with being the first disciple to recognize Jesus as the Messiah (Matt 16:13-20). In fact, it is difficult to imagine anyone in the churches of the New Testament more Christian than Peter, yet his childhood prejudice against Gentiles was so strong it took a special revelation for Peter to realize "that God shows no partiality, but in every nation anyone who fears him and does what is right is acceptable to him" (Acts 10:34-35). Both Peter and Paul learned through their experience with Jesus Christ that God was for all humankind, a belief that caused the church to define its mission to the whole world (Acts 15).

Throughout the New Testament, church members are expected to change from their culturally induced values and their self-centered concerns to become, as Paul wrote, "a new creation; everything old has passed away; see everything has become new" (2 Cor 5:17). Paul did not expect church members to change their beliefs or practices instantly, for he addressed most of his letters to people "who are called to be saints" (Rom 1:7). Paul's use of the word "saint" means church members who are in the process of being sanctified; that is, adults who are conscious of God working in their lives to do "his good pleasure" (Phil 2:13).

Hugh Kerr and John Mulder in their book *Conversions* have provided us with dramatic stories of Christians from New Testament times to our era who became aware of God's presence and what God wanted them to do.[4] In less dramatic ways adult classes can help adults clarify their beliefs about God and encourage them to translate those beliefs into practice. In the previous chapter I used two stories from a class on spiritual formation led by Lee Bowman. One of those adults, an active member of the church, learned Jesus' teaching on forgiveness. The other church member learned that in spite of his ego-centered personality, God loved him and was leading him to a new set of values.

Step 2: Have teachers coaching adults to experience faith in God. An effective way of teaching adults who are in the process of becoming more mature Christians is for teachers to assume some of the characteristics of a coach. The chief feature of coaches is that they know all about the game, but their role is to help the players play the game. Coaches also know that what the players experience in the game becomes the subject of the conversations they have with the players. If teachers of church school classes for adults had the traits of a good teacher and related themselves to the adults as a coach, the result would be more changed lives rather than more information about religion.

As a practical matter, how can teachers of adults incorporate some of the characteristics of a coach? The answer is to connect the experiences adults are having with the beliefs of the church. One way is to form a class on spiritual formation, as Lee Bowman did, for adults who are ready to examine their beliefs with peers and are ready to change their lifestyle. In teaching the Bible the teacher can ask members of the class to give their interpretation of how the passage relates to them. The following suggestions provide other simple ways of using experience as the bridge between belief and practice.

When teachers use their experience to illustrate the meaning of some belief, they also encourage members of the class to connect theology with life.

Allowing time to discuss connections between beliefs and practice during class time rather than at the end of the class invites members to apply the teacher's coaching to their situation.

Some topics, especially those that deal with Christian ethics, can be quickly related to adults' beliefs by the teacher asking groups of four or five to discuss the matter for a short time. The reports of the small groups to the whole class become the data to be discussed by everyone. This method is seldom used because Protestants do not have uniform opinions about ethical issues such as abortion; when to use military force; laws regarding preferential treatment based on a person's ethnic, racial, or gender status; ordination of homosexuals; or treatment of homeless people. Avoidance of these and other ethical issues that relate to the welfare of the community is a serious matter. Given the complexity of these issues, we should not expect Christians to agree on solutions. We should, however, learn how to discuss the issues so that different perspectives are considered in the mood of, "What does God want us to be and do in relation to the ethical issue?" There are few places in American society other than the church where adults can voice their beliefs about ethical issues, be listened to with respect, and together with peers be open to change.[6]

Most churches I know sponsor a variety of community resources, such as shelters for the homeless, halfway houses for persons released from prisons, Habitat for Humanity, various kinds of support groups, after-school programs for latchkey kids, or daycare centers. In conversations with adults who work as volunteers in these enterprises, I have heard stories of religious experience that strengthen the volunteers' faith, yet I have never heard these experiences shared with an adult class. This oversight is because we are trained to think that church classes are to be about only the substance of theology or Bible rather than the experiences adults are having as they live by their faith. Occasional reporting by adults who work in church-sponsored agencies that serve human needs would be an excellent way to teach this principle: "for just as the body without the spirit is dead, so faith without works is also dead" (Jas 2:26).

There is a secondary form of experience that teachers often use to present a generic human situation to which Christian doctrines apply. A brief section of a videotape of a television program or a movie may focus attention on an issue, an ethical problem, or a dramatic event that relates to the lives of church members. Using episodes from videotapes makes class discussion objective so everyone in the class can relate to them according to their understanding of Christian beliefs.

Occasionally a play or a well-advertised movie shown on television will contain scenes that support or challenge fundamental Christian beliefs. If a large percentage of an adult class sees the play or the television show, it should be discussed. The church has a responsibility to critique any play, movie, or television show that relates to Christian faith and morals. Support for the Christian doctrine of human sinfulness is clearly seen in *The Visit*, a play by Friedrich Duerrenmatt. This play is a realistic account of how sin emerges spontaneously in ordinary people when their financial interests are at stake. The play relates sin to human pride as theologians do, yet there is no reference to the Bible or theology. This secular description of human nature includes leaders of the church, for at the end of the play a priest blesses the mob as it is about to murder a well-respected citizen in order to be rewarded by a wealthy woman seeking revenge.[7] The challenge to Christian beliefs about morals—how people should relate to each other—is in many of the most popular sitcoms, music designed for teenagers, novels, and movies. Part of adult Christian education should be an analysis of the parts of American culture that support or challenge Christianity.

PARENTS INSTRUCTING CHILDREN

Parents are the first and most effective teachers of Christianity to their children. Recent research on children's mental development, summarized in chapters 2 and 3, provides us with abundant evidence that the way parents relate and what they say to their children provide the feelings and information out of which children form primitive images of God. This means two complex processes are going on at the same time. One process is the parents' struggle to become more mature in their faith. Parents' participation in congregational worship and educational programs should aid and support them in this lifelong endeavor. The second process is the parents' role in helping children develop adequate ideas of God and a set of behavior patterns that relate their children to other people. How can congregations help parents in their role as the first teachers of religious faith?

First, congregations should help parents understand that every aspect of their relationship with a child from birth on is important for the child's Christian faith. The establishment and growth of faith and knowledge follow a pattern related to a child's mental and emotional development. The sources of faith are in the sentiments (emotionally charged attitudes) that are formed in the first three or so years from a child's relation to parents. During that same time, a moral code (right and wrong behavior) is being formed that the child begins to talk about by age four. Then in middle childhood, as illustrated in chapter 3, children begin to use their reasoning ability to make sense of their beliefs.

Although there is a sequential order in children's development of faith in God, we should not absolutize it. Faith in God is rooted in feelings and thought, which means each child's development of faith is a part of that child's story. In chapter 2 I recalled Russell Baker's story. He became an atheist at age five because his father died. He had been taught that God caused things to happen;

therefore he would no longer believe in God. Compare Baker's response to a student in one of my classes who reported an identical experience. Her father died when she was five, so she decided she would no longer respect God. She liked Jesus and continued to go to Sunday school and church, but all through her childhood, youth, college, and early marriage she related to Jesus, not God. Then she had a baby. Somehow through that birth experience she became reconciled to God, felt a call to ministry, and entered seminary. She was ordained and became pastor of a church. We must remember that individuals form images of and relationships to God out of their *interpretation* of their experience. The presuppositions that interpret the meaning of experiences are usually formed in early childhood.

I have been using the word *nurture* more often than *education* because nurture connotes a relationship between people as well as direct instruction. There is considerable overlap between these two words, but *nurture* more clearly connects the act of instruction to life situations. Parents' acts of nurturing, for example, take place in relation to a problem, an event, a question, or how a child should act or speak in a certain specific situation. Parents do hundreds of nurturing acts every day, and the way parents justify or explain what they say or do becomes part of children's understanding of what to believe and how to act in relation to other people. Nurturing is thus unsystematic, but because it is centered in life situations it shapes a child's attitudes and values and provides knowledge about many things. *Education* can also mean what I have attributed to the word *nurture*, but too often *education* conveys the notion of teaching in a classroom. Regardless of the word used, what is important for the spiritual formation of children is parents who respect them from birth, as the parents model and explain the Christian way of life.

Second, congregations should plan to help parents create and maintain a Christian influence in the home. The family is more than a place to raise children. It is an extremely complex social institution where people of various ages and concerns are constantly interacting with each other. The adults in a family reveal the meaning of their religious faith as they deal with the demands of work, respond to ethical problems in a variety of situations, spend their time and money, participate in the worship and mission of their church, set roles for their children, voice opinions about political and social issues, and, perhaps, decide what obligations they have to their aging parents or relatives.

The church's concern for the welfare of the family is not new. What is new, as described in chapter 1, is the shift in American society from the Protestant evangelical ethos of the 1800s and early 1900s that supported family values to a culture that is becoming increasingly secular. As a result there is considerable tension in families between Christian and secular values that come into the home from sources such as television, the workplace, schools, neighbors, children's friends, magazines, music attractive to teenagers, movies, and community activities scheduled on Sundays. Since the family is the one place where parents can control their responses to this clash of values, church leaders have a renewed interest in the family as the primary place where the practice of Christian values becomes instructive.

How congregations can help parents form and sustain a Christian family life under modern conditions is difficult to imagine. Parents prefer to send their children to a Sunday school for Christian education. Church leaders have few examples of a ministry to families and little time or energy to test ways this might be done. If, however, church leaders realized that family life is the most influential factor in the development of children's faith in God and Christian values, they would start there to build a Christian education program.[8] Guidance is available to help congregations plan a family-centered program. A new journal, *Family and Community Ministries: Empowering Through Faith*, is dedicated to helping church leaders in every phase of this form of ministry.[9] Diana Garland, former editor of this journal, has written a book that covers every aspect of ministry to families. She includes in this book a long section on "Planning and Leading Family Ministry."[10]

Dorothy Bass and others have sponsored a movement under the banner of "Practicing our Faith." This movement is theologically based, but, rather than discussing theology in a rational matter, they want to help church members deepen their faith by living as their faith expects them to live. For example, Bass has proposed that church members discover the religious value of Sunday as a day for relaxation and reflection about our life in relation to our Christian beliefs. Aside from the merit of this movement, it is a good illustration of how this natural pattern of influence works. The congregation through worship, sermon, and classes for all age groups identifies Sunday as a special day. Adults, in their way, plan and celebrate Sunday in harmony with what the congregation supports. Parents explain to their children why they live in a certain way on Sunday.[11]

Lewis Sherrill, to whom this book is dedicated, was once asked, "How can one even ever know if a congregation has a successful Christian education program?" Sherrill replied, "Assume you are sitting in the balcony of a church just behind a man and his son who is about seven or eight years old. It is communion Sunday and the minister is beginning to distribute the bread and wine. The boy turns to his father and asks, what is the minister doing? The father gives the boy a rather good, short, explanation of what communion is and what it means for the boy to participate. If that happens, then that church has a good Christian education program."

Third, congregations should continue or expand all the congregation-based programs and activities they have that support family-centered religious instruction. The traditional way for churches to help parents is to provide classes for parents. These classes interpret the roles of parents in forming children's religious mentality, serve as a place where parents can support each other's efforts to do Christian education in the home, and supply parents with books and leaflets on childcare. Protestant publishers have well-edited picture books of Bible stories for children. If parents did no more than read a section of one of these Bible picture books to a child at bedtime, discuss the story, and conclude with a prayer, it would be a major contribution to that child's faith in God.

A children's catechism is one of the oldest and most widely used booklets for religious instruction in the home. Both Luther and Calvin wrote catechisms for children. The purpose was to provide a simple outline of basic Christian beliefs in question-and-answer format. Parents were expected to use the questions to start a discussion with their children so children could understand the belief in their own words and relate it to their experience. Unfortunately the catechism became something to memorize, often for a reward. Thus the catechetical method was boring and it encouraged children to think religion is correctly worded doctrine rather than a relation to

God. Recently the Presbyterian Church (U.S.A.) produced a children's version of its new catechism, *Belonging to God: A First Catechism.* In order for it to be used in the home as well as in church schools, a handbook, *We Are the Family of God: Conversations about the Catechism,* was prepared. This handbook helps parents use the questions as topics of conversation in the family.[12]

CHURCH INSTRUCTION OF CHILDREN AND YOUTH

This strategy of Christian education, based on the pattern of influence, continues the Sunday school and other agencies of instruction of children and youth. The role of the traditional agencies, however, changes from being the primary source of instruction to being a support and supplement for the instructions provided by parents and for what is learned from participation in the life and work of the congregation.

Childcare. Many churches have weekday childcare programs. Regardless of the ages of children enrolled, churches have an excellent opportunity to include religious songs, brief Bible lessons, and stories that illustrate Christian beliefs at some time during the hours the children are under church care. In addition, some carefully selected child guidance literature can be offered to parents.

Sunday School. Because the Sunday school is an agency of religious instruction the church controls, it is the standard Protestant effort to communicate the gospel to children and youth. During the past hundred years, denominational boards of Christian education, with the help of educators and biblical scholars, have developed excellent curriculum materials for every grade level in the Sunday schools of different-sized churches. Also, conference and training courses for teachers are vigorously promoted. The Sunday school is well established and should be supported because, even with only one hour per week, it has a remarkable influence on children.

Youth Instruction. Sunday school attendance decreases with age. The most rapid decrease is in the teen years as children gain more independence in the use of their time and they find more interesting things to do. Few churches have Sunday school classes for youth after high school, for they have gone to college, obtained jobs, entered military service, or in some other way achieved semi-independent status. When young people are about twelve to eighteen years old, congregations have, in addition to the Sunday school, two opportunities for religious instruction: confirmation and youth groups.

Many Protestant churches have a tradition of confirmation. The confirmation process, usually scheduled in the mid-teen years, includes a study of basic Christian beliefs, requirements for church membership, meaning of the sacraments, congregational polity, and an invitation to make a public confession of faith in Christ. The study portion of the process varies from six weeks to several years in a special class. Often an adult member of the congregation is assigned to each teenager as a "special friend" who goes with the youth through the whole experience. If the teenagers decide to make a profession of faith, it is in a special Sunday worship service where each one states an allegiance to Christ and the church that carries on Christ's ministry. Often each confirmand is given a Bible or some other item to mark the time and place of their pledge of allegiance to Christ.

Every aspect of the confirmation process is a learning experience. The instruction in fundamental beliefs is intellectual. The feeling of the congregation as a community is from the "special friend." A sense of self-affirmation emerges as one stands before family and friends and declares one's beliefs. For some teenagers the confirmation process clarifies the values they will use in making a vocational choice. Because the confirmation process is such a learning experience, congregations should do everything they can to make it memorable.

Next to the Sunday school and confirmation, the most important agency for church instruction of teenagers is a peer group. During the teen years, unique physical, social, and mental changes take place. Physically, children become adult in size and acquire the potential for reproduction. Socially, adolescents are expected to prepare for adulthood, select a vocation, be legally accountable for their behavior, make good grades in school, and keep out of trouble. Mentally, at about age sixteen, they are able to do abstract reasoning and make more mature judgments about social and political issues. This enormous shift in status and responsibility takes place during years when young people yearn for independence yet are dependent on their parents for all their needs and wants such as use of a car, financial support, and whatever freedom they can negotiate regarding dating and entertainment. As a result, most teenagers experience a certain amount of tension with their parents.

Some adolescents are able to move rather smoothly through the teen years, but the typical individual feels the need to associate with peers who are going through the same experience. Peer groups are a safe place to voice their frustrations, to offer plans and ideas that will be respected, to get information about relations with the opposite sex, and to test judgments about behavior in specific social situations. Peer groups will be formed, and for a time they will be very influential as teenagers move slowly into young adulthood. If congregations can provide peer groups (youth groups) for their teenagers or for other teenagers who have similar values, it will be of lasting benefit. Although church-sponsored peer groups seldom offer classes, they provide learning experience through the activities they sponsor and a fellowship of peers under the guidance of adults who model Christian maturity.[13]

NOTES

[1] If the reader desires to study the forms of Christian instruction that emerged in different eras, the following may be helpful for starting such an inquiry: Lewis J. Sherrill, *The Rise of Christian Education* (New York: The Macmillan Company, 1944); Kenneth O. Gangel and Warren S. Benson, *Christian Education: Its History and Philosophy* (Chicago: Moody Press, 1983), which begins with a listing of historical sources; James E. Reed and Ronnie Prevost, *History of Christian Education* (Nashville: Broadman & Holman Publishers, 1993), which begins with a preview of education in Greece and Rome because each of these cultures influenced some forms of Christian education.

[2] For a more complete analysis of adult education in congregations, see John M. Hull, *What Prevents Christian Adults from Learning?* (London: SCM Press, 1985).

[3] *The Kerygma Program*, developed by Presbyterians, is located at 300 Mt. Lebanon Blvd., Pittsburgh, PA, 15234. Information about the United Methodist Church *Disciple Bible Study* can be obtained toll free at (800) 672-1789 or by fax, (615) 749-6049. *The Bethel Series*, developed by Lutherans, is the work of Adult Christian Education Foundation, Box 8398, Madison, WI, 53708.

[4] Hugh T. Kerr and John M. Mulder, *Conversions* (Grand Rapids: William B. Eerdmans Publishing Co., 1983).

[5] These steps are general principles that may help church leaders develop a more effective adult education program. A much more detailed and practical process for developing an adult education ministry has been prepared by Diana Butler Bass. It is titled *Creating Congregational Formation for Vital Churches* and is available on the Internet: http://www.congregationalresources.org/adultfaith/pl.asp.

[6] Beth Ann Gaede, "Congregations: Talking about Homosexuality: Dialogue on a Difficult Issue," *Congregations*, Nov.–Dec. 1998, 4-8.

[7] Friedrich Duerrenmatt, *The Visit* (New York: Random House, 1956).

[8] Because a family is a dynamic interaction of individuals, each of whom has a unique set of needs and interests, it is a complicated place for ministry. If a church plans to employ a person to work directly with families as a place of Christian nurture, that person should have, in addition to the regular training for ministry, special education in family counseling. Such training, normally a Master of Arts degree, is offered in many universities and some seminaries.

[9] *Family Ministry: Empowering Through Faith* is published four times a year by the Louisville Presbyterian Theological Seminary, 1044 Alta Vista Rd., Louisville, KY, 40205-1798.

[10] Diana Garland, *Family Ministry: A Comprehensive Guide* (Downers Grove: InterVarsity Press, 1999), 367-515. A short, practical guide for a church planning a family ministry is by Joelene L. Roehlkepartain, "Innovative Ways to Build an Effective Family Ministry," *Family Ministry: Empowering Through Faith* 15/4 (2001): 12-20.

[11] Dorothy C. Bass, ed., *Practicing Our Faith* (San Francisco: Jossey-Bass Publishers, 1997); Dorothy C. Bass, *Receiving the Day* (San Francisco: Jossey-Bass Publishers, 2000); Miroslav Volf and Dorothy C. Bass, eds., *Practicing Theology* (Grand Rapids: Wm. B. Eerdmans Publishing Co., 2002). See also C. Ellis Nelson, "Spiritual Formation: A Family Matter," *Family Ministry: Empowering through Faith* 20/3 (Fall 2006): 13-28. This article is a commentary on the Shema, written to show parents how their practice of faith in God at home influences their children.

[12] Ann Reed Held and Sally Stockley Johnson, *We Are the Family of God: Family Conversations about the Catechism* (Louisville: Geneva Press, 1998).

[13] A congregational approach to the Christian education of youth involves much more than the agencies of instruction I mentioned. For a more comprehensive discussion, see my *Helping Teenagers Grow Morally* (Louisville: Westminster/John Knox Press, 1992).

DISCUSSION GUIDE

PRELIMINARY

Since the purpose for studying this book is to help a congregation change its Christian education strategy, a class for this purpose should be formed.

A steering committee of three or more people who are concerned about Christian education and also have considerable knowledge about the life and work of the congregation should be selected. This committee should meet well in advance of the first class to:

- select a leader skilled in leading discussion,
- recruit adults for the study,
- select a time and place for the class meeting, and
- order enough books so that each member of the class will have a copy.

This steering committee should meet briefly after each class to identify and solve any problems that arise.

The following suggestions are for an introductory class plus one class for each of the seven chapters. The steering committee may decide to hold an additional class at the end to discuss ways their congregation should modify its program for nurturing disciples. If so, suggestions for that added meeting are included.

FIRST CLASS: INTRODUCTION

Introduce the steering committee and the person who will lead the discussions. If the class has been authorized by congregational officers or a committee, share that information.

Explain the reason for the course: "We may need a more effective Christian education program. This course supports the Sunday school and other church educational agencies as necessary but as not sufficient for the secular society in which we live. At the end of our study, we may want to recommend some changes in our educational work. To help us work through this important aspect of our congregational life, we have this book, *Growing Up Christian: A Congregational Strategy for Nurturing Disciples.*"

Hand out the books. Have everyone turn to the introduction. Read each paragraph and then say a bit more and ask for questions about the paragraph. Explain that members of the class are expected to read each chapter before it is scheduled to be discussed. Urge each member to write questions or comments as they read each chapter and to bring them for the class to consider.

There should be some time left to have the class turn to the first chapter. Explain that this is the longest chapter because it is necessary that we understand why the Sunday school was a success in the 1800s and why it is not sufficient today. Call attention to the two charts (pages 19 and 32) that describe the "patterns of influence." Ask the class to give special attention to the chart on page 32 that illustrates our situation today. If anyone disagrees with this chart, request that he or she draw a chart that better reflects how our culture influences our children. If time remains, have the class start silent reading of chapter one.

CHAPTER 1: WHY THE STRATEGY OF THE 1800S IS INADEQUATE FOR THE 2000S

This chapter uses history to show how culture influences the thoughts, beliefs, and lifestyles of the rising generation. If you think an introduction to this idea is necessary, you could start with the question, "Has anyone lived or traveled in a country greatly different from the United States?" If so, have these people give examples of the cultural differences. If no one volunteers, ask for help in noting the differences between American and Arabian nations. When some significant differences have been noted, ask, "How do children learn to be American or Arabian?" It should become clear that the first influence is the family, which is informed and supported by the community in which they live. After such an introduction, you can skim over the 1800s, noting as you go how people were influenced by the economic and social situation in which they lived. If people have brought questions or comments about this section, deal with them as you skim through the text. Give special attention to the chart on page 19 that attempts to put the 1800s in graphic terms.

Depending on their ages, members of the class may be acquainted with the social and cultural changes of the past twenty-five years. The discussion about culture change should be lively. Questions such as, "How have the computer and cell phone influenced children and teenagers?" may help the class realize the power of environmental influence. The chart on page 32 shows the churches with little ability to change our social situation. Is this a correct assessment? Did members of the class change the chart? If so, ask for the changes. Does the strength of the evangelical and megachurch movements have much effect on American society?

Chapter 2: Parents: The Primary Source for Children's Images of God

The purpose of chapter 1 was to show the way culture helps or hinders the church's efforts to nurture disciples of Jesus Christ. The purpose of this chapter is to describe recent research about how much infants learn in their first three years, including primary images of God. We must, therefore, attend to the role of the family as a major factor in what children learn in their first few years.

The first several pages of this chapter describe briefly the rapid way a baby's brain develops. Was there anything in this review that surprised you? If babies' brains develop so rapidly, should we wait until they are old enough to go to Sunday school to tell them about God? Anne-Marie Rizzuto, a psychiatrist, has studied the way children form mental images of God. She is cited on pages 48-50 as saying this process begins at birth through the parents' feelings toward the infant. Rizzuto means that feelings about life start with birth, and they become the bases on which the infant develops a primary image of God. Does this make sense to you? If so, then a congregational Christian education program should provide ways to help parents understand that they are the first, and for a while, the only source of religious nurture for their children. Ask if anyone has an idea of how their congregation could help parents in this regard.

CHAPTER 3: FAMILY AND COMMUNITY: THE SECONDARY SOURCE FOR CHILDREN'S IMAGES OF GOD

Ask if any person in the class knows a child who developed an image of God like the children did as noted on pages 37-52. If so, ask those persons to report how the child described God. Discuss each story, pointing out what influenced the child to have his or her image of God. If no one volunteers to share a story, turn to the stories on pages 56-63. Select two or three stories for discussion. Include story number 4 because it illustrates how important the Sunday school is for children as their thinking matures. In general terms, what a person has been taught and experienced about religion in childhood remains with them (pages 63-65). During the teen years there is a testing about what a person has learned. What idea of God that results from teenage testing is not predictable.

From a Christian perspective we know that one's faith in God must be a conscious realization of God's presence and guidance (page 66). We will study the role of the congregation in helping Christians move through their teen and adult years with such a knowledge of God's presence and expectations in chapter 4.

At this point, note that many Christians who were confirmed as church members in their teen years become nominal Christians. They maintain church membership, lead honest and useful lives, but they put success, political power, social prestige, or some form of acclaim ahead of a Christian lifestyle. Sometimes an event happens that causes them to return to their knowledge of God from their childhood. They then rapidly change their lives or they reconnect to God. Ask, "Is there anyone in the class with such a story to tell?" If not, use the two stories on pages 68-70. Such stories show the importance of childhood Christian education.

CHAPTER 4: THE PERSUASIVE POWER OF CONGREGATIONS

Remind the class that this chapter and the remaining ones contain practical suggestions to help a congregation develop a more effective Christian education strategy. Repeat the strategy in outline form. This strategy starts with the question, "What influences people to be religious?" The answer is (1) the community (congregation) to which the people belong, (2) the education and leadership of adults, (3) the practice of religion in one's family, and (4) church-sponsored instruction much as the Sunday school.

Start the class discussion with thanksgiving for our constitutional right for religious freedom. Except for a few laws regarding public safety and car parking, the congregation is one place where we have complete control over what we believe, say, and do.

Call attention to the goal of discipleship, especially the paragraph on the bottom of page 75 that insists that character traits and beliefs are like two sides of one coin. What is your class's response?

Ask, "What parts of congregational life help make it such a powerful source of influence?" After people mention items such as music, prayer, sermon, fellowship, projects to help the poor, guidance for moral and ethical issues, and so on, ask the class to respond to identify two or three parts that are most influential.

Probably the sharing of beliefs is the reason congregations shape the mentality of their members (pages 77-79).

Have the class turn to the bottom of page 81 and silently read through page 82. Start a discussion by asking a cluster of questions such as, Does reading this page help you understand Paul's conversion? Do you relate to Paul's statement that he gave up childish thoughts about God (1 Cor 13:11) when he became a man and understood—with the help of a congregation—that God was gracious? Could Paul have made such a drastic change in belief without the support of a congregation?

If time remains, you could ask if the three beliefs listed on pages 85-87 are sufficient to hold a congregation together.

CHAPTER 5: INFORMAL PROCESS OF NURTURING.

First, explain ethos as a process of nurturing. Ethos means the characteristics or distinguishing attitudes, values, and activities of a congregation. Some congregations formalize their ethos in a written statement. Although other congregations do not adopt a written statement, they have characteristics that most members like.

Because congregations consist of people who have similar beliefs and lifestyles, just being a part of the congregation is nurturing as members influence each other through conversation, prayers, discussions in classes, and in whatever projects the congregation sponsors. So the dynamic interaction of church members creates an ethos that is a major influence for defining and supporting a Christian lifestyle.

Second, have the class turn to pages 92-95. Pick out a few examples of a distinctive congregational ethos, such as Don Browning (page 94), Gary Dorsey (page 94), or Nile Harper (page 95). Point out how the ethos would attract and nurture members.

Third, turn the attention of the class to the ethos of their congregation. One way would be to have a general discussion with the hope that everyone would participate. Perhaps a better method would be to ask the class members spontaneously to form groups of two or three to identify what they consider to be the ethos of their congregation. After 10 to 15 minutes, call the class together and get a report from each group. Summarize the reports into a few general characteristics.

Fourth, the last section in this chapter, pages 97-99, assumes that congregations do a self-analysis that might lead to a change of mission. Such a change may cause conflict. Ask, "What do you think of the two principles on page 97 that might help a congregation make a change without too much conflict?"

CHAPTER 6: FORMAL PROCESSES OF NURTURING: WORSHIP AND SERMON

Pastors are called or appointed to lead a congregation based on their training, experience, and personality. It is understood that pastors are in charge of worship, and they preach according to their judgment of what is appropriate for the congregation. Given this expectation, why should we discuss worship and sermon as a part of Christian education? We do so because this book interprets Christian education as a form of nurturing people to "love . . . God with all your heart, soul, and mind" (Matt 22:37). This chapter, therefore, suggests a few ways the worship and sermon aspects of congregational life are a nurturing influence.

One way to help the pastor is to realize that every aspect of church life should be related to bridging the gap between Christian beliefs and our lifestyle. Pages 101-104 will help readers understand why narrowing the gap is a job in which all church members should be engaged. This participation in worship and absorbing sermons is a way to grow in a Christian lifestyle.

Another suggestion is to help the pastor have an opportunity to teach youth and adult classes. The examples on pages 105-106 are of pastors who took the initiative to teach a Bible class. Youth and adult classes could take the initiative to ask the pastor to teach a section of whatever book they are studying. The point is to develop a community in which people know and respect each other. Being with the pastor in a class should result in church members developing a sympathetic relationship with the pastor and the pastor's work. Question: "Are there other ways church members can arrange events through which the pastor can gain rapport?"

The sermon is a direct effort to inspire and instruct church members. Pastors select sermon topics and a style of preaching. Except for making audio copies of the sermon for members who were absent, the influence of each sermon ends. There are, however, two ways to extend the life and influence of a sermon. One way is for the sermon to be discussed in small groups. On page 108 and in the middle of page 110 I note that I have seldom seen a plan for church members' discussion of sermons last very long. Question: "Does anyone in the class know a church where the sermon is regularly discussed in small group? If so, what is your judgment about the church's value?"

A second way to extend the influence of a sermon is for it to be connected to some part of the congregation's program. Examples of how ministers connected a sermon with the youth groups are described in the middle of page 108 and page 109. Ask: "Can members of the class recall sermons that were connected with the ongoing work of the congregation? What kinds of sermons are most helpful; that is, sermons that you recall as you go about your daily activities?"

Probably the most influenced and memorable speech from a pulpit is a testimony from a church member about God's presence and guidance. Such testimonies were common for hundreds of years but have now almost disappeared. Beginning on page 111, Lee Bowman's reintroduction of this form of sharing the gospel (good news) is described. Question: "Has anyone in the class been in a church where testimonies were shared by the whole congregation? Has anyone been in an adult class where members shared their faith journey?" Using the replies from these questions or testimonies on pages 111-14, ask members of the class what influence such testimonies might have on their religious beliefs.

CHAPTER 7: FORMAL PROCESSES OF NURTURING: INSTRUCTION

The "inconvenient truth" of this book is that becoming a disciple of Jesus Christ involves the affections as well as the mind. The affections/emotions that motivate our behaviors are acquired through our relations to our parents, friends, mentors, and the groups to which we belong. Thus, any effort to communicate the Christian faith to the rising generation must attend to the way in which children and youth are influenced. The way proposed in this book is listed on page 118. Ask: "Do you agree with this way? If not, how would you prioritize the four sources of influence?"

The first order of influence is the congregation. Because this source of influence is basic to all others, we devoted chapters 4 and 5 to this topic.

The second order of influence is adult education. Because the Sunday worship is adult-centered and the sermon is inspirational and instructive, they have been discussed in chapter 6. In that chapter we noted the indirect instruction of adults. In this chapter we discuss the direct teaching of adults. According to this strategy, the teaching of adults should have top priority because adults create the congregation's ethos and parents influence the nurture of their children. But for reasons listed on page 119, most congregations do not emphasize adult education. This is a serious mistake. Question: "Were the practical suggestions for planning a more extensive adult education program (suggested on pages 120-21 or the listing of opportunities for adult education on pages 121-23) of any help for enlarging the adult education in your church?" Narrowing the gap between beliefs and lifestyle, noted in chapter 6 on pages 101-104, is a condition that should be discussed in an adult class. Ask: "What do you think of the suggestions on pages 123-27 as a teaching style for this condition?"

The third order of influence is the family. This location and style of teaching is of greater influence than the Sunday school. The section on parents' role in nurturing faith in God, pages 127-31, contains references on how a congregation can plan a program that will help families teach their children about God. One suggestion is that churches have someone visit parents in their homes to encourage them to practice prayer and to read Bible passages and Christian stories to their children. The home visitor could also leave some print materials or DVDs to support this teaching of Christianity at home. Ask: "Would such a plan work for your church?"

The fourth source of influence is instruction in various kinds of schooling including summer camps, conference, and mission trips. The methods of instruction are well established and must be continued. Moreover, these forms of instruction often include experiences such as conversations, role modeling, sharing of personal religious experience, work projects such as Habitat for Humanity, and trips of various kinds that help shape children and teenagers' affections.

CHAPTER 8: WHAT SHOULD WE DO BETTER TO NURTURE DISCIPLES?

Although there are general characteristics that can be noted in almost all congregations, each congregation is unique according to its history, size, location, budget, buildings, sense of mission, and style of leadership. If this study of how people are influenced to be Christian has any value for your congregation, it will be necessary for members of the class to apply the proposed strategy to the unique features of your church.

First, "do no harm." Almost any effort to change the educational program of a congregation will meet with some resistance. Changes have a better chance of surviving if they are done as "disjointed incrementalism," mentioned on page 97. Also, remember that a congregation is a community to which people belong because of its beliefs and its characteristics. Thus, changes should be made slowly and with full knowledge and approval of the church. However, changes suggested in this book should be fairly easy to accomplish because they do not require any changes in the Sunday school or other agencies of education and because congregations have a strong desire to nurture disciples effectively.

One way to take an inventory of the congregation's Christian education program would be to follow the three sources of influence summarized on pages 131-32.

The most significant source of influence is the life and work of the congregation. This influence is under the control of the pastor and the elected officers, so any ideas the class has about this source of influence should be referred to them. For example, members of this class may have ideas as to how children and teenagers could be included in more of the congregation's projects.

The next most significant source of influence is the adults because they are the church's officers, teachers, and parents. Yet adult education as a well-developed program is often neglected. Take time to list all the adult classes and their enrollment. How many adults are not enrolled in any study of the Bible or theology? Does the present set of classes for adults cover all the needs and interests of adults?

The most significant source of influence on the religious life of children and teenagers is their parents and their family situation. There are many ways our secular society promotes its values to children through schools, TV, cell phones, books, computers, and magazines. The home, however, is one place where parents have considerable control.

We know from chapter 2 that children will form primary images of God by the age of three. Parents need guidance and support as they try to establish a Christian perspective. Yet a ministry to the home is neglected by most congregations. Does your congregation have a class for parents? Does your congregation have a psychologist available to help parents with difficult situations? Can your congregation employ someone—a pastor or layperson—to visit parents in their home in order to help them establish a regular time for prayers and reading from the Bible?

The fourth source of influence is from the Sunday school, youth groups, and various kinds of activities for children and teenagers. These well-known and established sources of influence are usually under the supervision of a committee and are well managed. Unless there are problems with these efforts to nurture disciples, they should be supported.